The Half-Built House

On The Hill

The Half-Built House
On The Hill

Big Daddy Sun
Ten Thousand Flies

Marriage, Motherhood, and Madness

a memoir

Laurie Corn

ISBN-13: 9781513651644

to my children Ben and Sami
who lived with me through all this
and still love me

and to the flies. . .

a persistent presence
the measure of my sanity
the gauge of my
spiritual evolution

Contents

Foreword

1995

I awoke with a thick cord of pain in my left temple, familiar reminder of my heritage—a long line of authentic Russian pain all the way from the Baltic Sea. In the mornings when we sat at our round table in the breakfast nook before going off to school, my mother would sometimes drift into the room in slow motion, drop into a chair, and sit with a warm cup of coffee pressed to her temple. I, myself, have spent many nights sitting, hand pressed to my head, wrapped in a blanket like a mummy, waiting for morning. I learned great patience in this way.

I have taken my headache to The White Raven, "best little pourhouse" in Felton, California. Felton is a turn of the century logging town in the San Lorenzo Valley where much of the wood was milled for the rebuilding of San Francisco after the great fire of 1906. This is redwood country, and the gently rolling mountains surrounding the Valley, green and lush with redwoods, madrones, and pines, are visible from almost anywhere. We are mountain people, a good many of us living in the backwoods up winding roads, along inland rivers and streams. We have chickens, goats and horses and drive big trucks. In winter we are busy surviving the fierce mountain rains.

Six miles down Highway 9 from Felton is Santa Cruz, a progressive and prosperous city on the surfer coast of central California, complete with a historic boardwalk that once hosted the Miss California pageants until the wave of 60s feminism put an end to all that. It is the seat of county government, the site of a plethora of coffee shops, music venues, and indie film theaters. On two thousand acres of forested hills, canyons, farmland and fields overlooking the Pacific Ocean, is spread the ever-expanding campus of the University of California at Santa Cruz.

My home in the San Lorenzo Valley, fortunately, is far removed from all of that. When I leave Santa Cruz and begin the winding drive through the forests of Highway 9 and when the first shaft of golden light slants rococo-like through the towering trees, it is a religious experience every time, and I am home again.

White Raven, I think my old friend The Muse and I have found ourselves a place to write. The headache is loosening its grip. Some of it floats above me mixing with the 90s new age music and the hearty aroma of fresh-brewed coffee.

That is how it began: a headache and a café—and my daughter Sami in her twenties, one day digging through a box of photographs, asking me about those days in the half-built house on the hill. Photographs when studied closely reveal much that is untold—photos such as the one of Sami clutching a big stuffed rabbit at the edge of the rubble-strewn living room without walls, with a look on her face that can only stir up mother-guilt, like mud churned up from a creek bed. Those pictures were boxed away for a reason.

And so it fell to me to find all the wrinkled and mildewed scraps of writing, shards of the 70s, and to rediscover what it was that happened. I already had the skeleton of the story—a book of poems and prose written in the 70s. Some of those original pieces are sprinkled like salt and pepper throughout this book; they hold the immediacy of an era redolent with the raw passion of the mountain hippie. We 70s hippies are legendary, aren't we, what with home birth, the sacred drugs, the music, and living in shacks like earthy peasants? We felt the impending era of technocracy, and milked our counterculture lifestyle for all it was worth.

But this is not a book celebrating the mythos of the hippie era. This book is more an elegy exposing, on a personal level, the underbelly of the 70s—the suffering of a trapped woman trying to be a wife, mother (and let's not forget, poet) in the squalor of a fly-infested trailer and a half-built house.

The White Raven
The White Raven where I spent many days writing has become a voice in this narrative. She is the present talking to the past. She is the savvy crone hovering, swooping in as a foil to the younger me of the 70s—cajoling, taunting, shaking her finger, asking questions—trying to make sense of my odyssey to the edge of sanity.

The Epilogue
Key to this writing is the Epilogue, holding answers to poignant questions and revealing what surprising things can happen when a dark spell is broken.

Beginnings

ONE

Eli, Eli

I pray that these things never end
The sand and the sea
The rush of the waters
The crash of the heavens
The prayer of the heart

Hebrew Prayer By Hanah Senesh
Jewish WWII Fighter, Hungarian Resistance

I think it is in the passing of the seasons that I am Home. When all else fails, there are the autumn leaves. There is the frozen pond in Ottawa Park. There is the budding dogwood tree in the front yard. There are June Bugs at Lake Erie.

My childhood is an endless kaleidoscope of seasons turning and turning. A young girl is darting perpetually around a backyard fenced by lilac bushes, catching lightning bugs in a jar until it is a glowing lantern in the dark, and then letting them go to rise up and hover like tiny helicopters in the thick muggy sea of night.

Turn the kaleidoscope—and she is raking fallen leaves with a widespreading rake into huge piles, then running and landing with her brothers and sisters in the crashing, sinking softness. Turn again—and she is sitting on the window seat of her knotty-pine bedroom looking down on the first snow of winter, everything marshmallow soft and round: the brick windowsill outside the breakfast nook, the street curb, the mounds suggesting garbage can or rock or tree root. And then on that first warm day of spring when she can leave her cardigan sweater at home, she is walking up the tree-arched street to Old Orchard Elementary feeling light and breezy and hopeful.

I was born a child of wartime. I remember the WWII years in black and white like the footage and photos of that era, except for the Victory Garden in brilliant color and the glass jars of preserved vegetables lining the shelves of our basement.

The horrors of that war did not touch me except as undercurrents and whispered voices. What I see is my young parents embracing in the hallway of the red brick bungalow on Powhattan Parkway. I see my mother in her tan gabardine slacks raking the Victory Garden and my tall, handsome father home from work, striding up the front walk, cold air surrounding him as he takes off his overcoat and reaches up to place his hat on the coat closet shelf.

My mother had a moonface—high Russian cheekbones, white powdered skin, eyes as blue and sparkling as an Indiana summer lake, and a smile painted Revlon "Cherries in the Snow." I see her moonface beaming down at me, as seen from a small face looking up. It was her moonface that seemed to promise: 'Everything is all right and will always be all right.'

My romantic fantasies are rooted in the 40s: in the dresses, the hats, the heroism, the music. I remember those war years in a cozy, comforting way because in my family everything was all right and would always be all right. That was the premise and that was the theme.

TWO

"To be born in peace, to be born in freedom
is only a matter of luck. . .and good geography."

- Grandma Fanya – Age 89

THEY CAME FROM RUSSIA—THE OLD ones—and in that dark other world are the seeds of my life. The Old World has tinged my blood; I have the imprints of memories that are not even mine.

In growing up I asked little about how my grandparents from Eastern Europe landed in America, more specifically "Toledo, America." Once they were here, they were here. It was just a fact of life that if you were Jewish, you had *bubbas* and *zedahs* who spoke with accents and who had modest, hard-working lives in urban America. They worked and saved so their sons (and maybe their daughters, but surely their sons) could learn violin or piano and later have a college education. We Jews are "the people of the book."

Czar Nicholas II. That is a name that rings through the collective memory of the Jews. At the turn of the century during the second wave of pogroms, the exodus of Jews from the Russian Pale intensified. With falsified passports they voyaged to America, and once the young men and women had settled and saved enough, they would send for the other family members. There is a direct link between me and this Czar. Czar Nicholas is the reason I am here.

Our blood was full of Russia, but our lives were what stretched in front of us and to the left and right. Yet, when I saw Fiddler on the Roof

I felt that I had walked those cobbled streets before and seen those old men standing in the courtyard rubbing their beards.

Those old men were transplanted from that Russian courtyard to the old *Shara Tzedek* Synagogue on Canton Avenue in Toledo. I sat with the women upstairs peering over the balcony rail as the men down below, wrapped in their white fringed *tallisim,* prayed to God and talked to each other, with God and the women looking down.

PART 1

The Midwest

THERE ARE STRETCHES OF LIFE that are smooth and even as the fields of Midwest, a sea of oats waving in the breeze, season following season—green into gold into sienna. There is more drama in the life of the beaver building a lodge, going in for winter, coming out again into spring. You are a duck in a flock of ducks. Your memories are the memories of the fox or the field mouse, one day melding into the next, and you hold quiet to the quick of your life—until the days of turbulence come, days when the winds of change stir like a warm storm with you at the quiet eye—and your restless soul is paying attention.

The Muse Child

In 1945 kindergarten was curtailed in the war effort, so private nursery schools sprang up everywhere. When I was four a brown station wagon came for me every day and drove me way out in the country to a grand old colonial house called Breldway. I see sunlight streaming through the windows of the playroom and leafy-green trees peeking in. Polly Potter led the band of triangles and bells and drums with a pout on her face that never changed. We played outside on slides and swings and sometimes we were led around the playground on a pony.

Kind Mrs. Courtney read stories and taught us French words and songs. I loved the taste of French inside my mouth. At story-telling time, Joyce would sit in back of me and play with my hair. Sometimes she pulled it, twisting it around, trying to make pigtails, and it always felt good.

The head of the school was a tall grey Witchlady, and the sunlit playroom and leafy-green trees grow murky shadows when I think of her. Every day after morning play they gave us lunch—green and yellow canned vegetables I could not eat: slimy spinach sitting in a wet pool, soft green beans with their terrible green bean smell, pale asparagus, limp and ugly. I knew that I would be sick if I ate them. My mother never made me, but the Witchlady, in her sharp and ringing voice, said I must, and every day she grew to hate me more.

She put me under the table where I watched the other children's feet, waiting for lunch to be over. One day she took me from my floor place under the table and put me in a small dark closet. Day after day I went to my closet, and the voices of the others faded away into the other world.

I never told on the Witchlady, not even to my mother. But the boy with the monkey face—I told him every day that I wouldn't be coming back again, and every day I would see his monkey face watching me.

The Witchlady broke into my privacy one day, and when my eyes could stand the light I saw her towering over me holding a birthday cake, all pink and white frosting. The glowing candles lit her gray face and she said, "This is what you would have had if you had eaten your vegetables."

She turned with her cake and the darkness closed in on me again. I heard the muffled birthday song outside the door.

I think in my closet I grew up faster than the others out there eating lunch.

There in the closet the Muse, herself a child, found me crouched in the corner, and touched me with a sweet soul sadness and a memory of total recall. Out of the purple darkness emerged the quintessence of what I came to call "My Laurie Me."

I felt the sadness in things: in the cold dreary sky full of circling birds, in the plaid dress folded away because it had become too small. The sadness of seeing from my window a strange lonesome dog walking in the middle of the road at night with no place to go.

> *White Raven,*
>
> *I can still go to Breldway, to the year four of my mind—every detail alive like a vivid waking dream that has the ring of a fairy tale. To morph the impressions of a tender virgin soul into an adult understanding or a personal myth that shapes your life—that is the stuff of the poet.*
>
> *Aristotle gave us the word "entelechy"—meaning that the potential becomes the actual. Just as the caterpillar is destined to become the butterfly, the vital force of the nascent soul directs the life of a person.*
>
> *The closet didn't make me a poet.*
>
> *The poet in me found a home in the closet.*

Toledo

T-O-L-E-D-O. Even the word Toledo is sturdy, solid, dependable. Rust Belt cities do not have frilly names: Detroit, Flint, Elyria, Dayton, Lima, Akron—names that make you think of large brick factories and railroad yards. Toledo is a port city situated on the mouth of the Maumee

River that flows into Lake Erie. It was, in its early days, a burgeoning giant of industry boasting some brewing companies, a potato chip manufacturer, Sealtest milk and ice cream in the days when chocolate, vanilla and strawberry were the only flavors, and significantly, the American Bicycle Company that made the "Toledo Steamer," one of the first autos. Later, of course, the Willy-Overland jeep company supplied most of the jeeps for WWII. By the time I was a teenager, the City was rich with its manufacture of glass, scales, spark plugs, and jeeps.

We were not rich. We were middle-class, and in those days middle-class meant prosperity. In the post-war years neighborhoods spread and businesses grew like mushrooms out of piles of scrap iron. There were fortunes to be made, and even if you had a small family business such as my father's jewelry and watch repair business, if you invested wisely, you passed "go" and collected $200 and the little houses were bought and placed like Monopoly pieces on square lots with a Buick in the driveway, evergreens in the front, and a fenced in backyard with a dog. There was no rush or urgency to life. One year expanded into the next as the kaleidescope of seasons turned.

When my mother's belly was swollen with the fourth baby we moved from the neighborhood of Indian-named streets—our own, Powhattan Parkway—to Old Orchard, a neighborhood with old English named streets like Middlesex and Barrington. My parents designed a ranch house on Drummond Road covered in used brick from the old Union Train Station and topped with a weathervane that was a rooster—a house that kept expanding and changing shape over the years as in a funhouse mirror, until there was room for all six children.

There are no more beautiful streets in all the world than the streets of Old Orchard where I walked to school every day. Not in Beverly Hills. Not anywhere. The branches of great leafy trees formed vaulted archways over the streets. Running through Old Orchard was Kenwood

Boulevard, lined with stone castles with turrets and leaded glass windows. My brother and the other boys on our street were the Knights of Drummond Road, each with sword and shield, and they fought regularly over Suzie Hanson, the blond blue-eyed one who lived next door.

My father was a Gregory Peck prince-of-a-father sitting for all eternity in his easy chair, pipe raised to his mouth. My mother was a fountain of beauty and goodness standing at the clothesline in a flowered wrap-around dress—a Norman Rockwell painting. In this perfect world you could count on the blue spruce trees to be laden with snow, the castle houses to be lined with blue Christmas lights, tobogganing in Ottawa Park, road trips to Washington at cherry blossom time, June barbeques, cottages and row boating at Pottowatome, Sunday school, piano lessons, Broadway musicals in Detroit. There was everything. Everything. Nothing was left out.

It is difficult for one not to conjure up some gothic serpentine spirit ready to spiral up out of all that goodness, some hidden awfulness that was repressed, but truly there was none. The worst of my father's rarely heard outbursts was, "Oh, for crying out loud!" My mother's version of swearing was "Oh peas!" In my family there was nary a raised voice. Because my parents got along so famously, six children grew up never learning to disagree, never armed with the tools of simple confrontation. How could any of us develop unhappiness antibodies if harmony was the natural state?

No wonder my Aunt Rose asked me: "How can you write a memoir? You had such an idyllic childhood." True, I am not Sylvia Plath or Anne Sexton—no suicidal poet. I had no lusty uncles, no grandfather with wandering fingers. I have lived through no reign of terror, escaped no European tyrant in the dark tunnel of night. I'm sorry. I apologize for my sweet, functional family, for the brick house on Drummond Road, for the birch tree Mom planted in the front yard, and winter snow walks, and June barbeques. I'm sorry.

White Raven,
Today, I am thinking of my mother. She is the real reason for our mythic childhood. Throughout time her moonface appeared, as dependable and familiar as the moon in the sky—her laughter rippling, her voice smooth and pearly. She glided through life, elegant as a swan. No waves. Just smooth parting of the water as she sailed along, queenly and dazzling. She was All Beauty. And now that she has sailed away, my mother is a beauty of the silent screen.

It is January, and raining hard. Rivulets of water wander haphazardly down the window by my table. Waterlogged locals sit around discussing the weather. They call this winter, but I know that after the rain a new crew cut of grass will spring up, and acacia trees will droop with mustard yellow blooms up and down the country roads. I don't try to understand.

I have lived more than half my life in California, yet I have made no attempt to excuse the absence of the seasons. Perhaps it is my Russian blood, this need for cyclical extremes. We people of Russian blood, we are Immigrants of the Soul—all of us.

In the Land of Childhood, grasses gave up and died in winter, buried by brown leaves, and not seen again until tiny shoots pushed through the ground, miraculous and green, in the spring thaw. It was a green more luminous than California green because it came out of nothing. Here, where it is 80 degrees in December and houses drip blue icicle Christmas lights, I am bereft.

Here—in the Land of the Lollipop Sun tracing its faithful path across the flawless blue, weathermen apologize for any symptom of weather: rain, wind, fog or drizzle. I am told: "There are four seasons here. You just have to pay attention. They are more subtle." I know. I know, but who wants subtle weather?

Here—in the land of "Beach Bettys" and surfer dogs I settled as an immigrant to a strange land settles, but in leaving the Land of Seasons I abandoned my past and my spirit became homeless.

The World Out There

If the closet at Breldway is what we call traumatic, as a small child I didn't know that. Although it shaped my life deeply in some ways—most importantly, the lifelong attraction to the vast, welcoming wilderness of solitude—my secret trip to the underworld was overridden by the absolute goodness that lived in the sanctuary of our home. But as it lived *only* in our home, I grew increasingly shy of the world out there. The world out there and I were in a standoff of mutual distrust.

Throughout my young life I would wonder what was expected of me. After all, I never asked to be born. Growing up in prosperous America, the easy choice would have been to glide through the seasons in the arms of a loving family, to do what was expected in that milieu. Instead, I had chosen Romantic Melancholia. I would never fit in. I would never be a duck in a row of ducks.

In middle school my self-consciousness was acute, incurable, and ridiculous. Once on my way to my piano lesson in downtown Toledo, I stepped off the bus and headed in the wrong direction. I was so afraid that turning around would look stupid, that I walked all the way around the block to correct the mistake.

In high school you could see me standing in the outfield praying that the ball would not fly in my direction. And batting was worse, everyone watching, judging. Batting good had somehow led to flirting good, being a cheerleader, getting voted to class office. And not batting good led to being shy and not knowing how to flirt and all the rest.

The ways of talking to boys were a locked secret and I didn't have the key. I was dateless, except for one fix-up with a college guy. My friends teased: "Now don't be a cold potato." I knew about petting, understood "going all the way," but I didn't know where one stopped and the other started. Nobody explained these things.

While the others were in love with football jocks or cool, black leather, slicked-back greasy-haired James Dean look-alikes, I was in deep love with my sixty-year-old French teacher, Pierre Pasquier. I would always wonder if he was my one truest love—he sixty and I sixteen. He came to me as shamanic love; a union immortal and familiar, as if I had known him through the centuries. He limped along with a wooden leg, a legacy of fighting for France in the Great War. To the other girls he was "Peg Leg Pierre." They were just too young; and I was just too old.

Small Frog in a Big Pond

In 1959, I transferred my shy and dateless life to the sprawling campus of the University of Michigan. In high school I had been an award-winning French student. Now, lost in the swarm of students from all over the country, I could barely pull a 'C.' I lived in Mary Markley Dorm for women. If a male student (or an empty beer can, for that matter) was found in your room it was grounds for suspension. Yet panty raids were legal, a sanctioned outlet for tension between the sexes. Hordes of boys would come tromping up the hill to the girls' dormitories shouting "To the Hill! To the Hill!" The girls would appear on balconies waving their panties and the boys would climb the building and capture them. The 50s were not over yet.

My popular roommate from Omaha decided one day that it was time for me to have a date. She fixed me up with a man named John. We started out in Drakes, a coffee shop with the world's best pecan sticky buns, and then moved on to his fraternity party. There was the usual struggle with conversation and general lack of fun. On leaving me at the door of Mary Marklee dorm he spoke these words: "You're not the kind of girl to date. You're the kind of girl to marry." I never saw him again.

At the time those words hit me like rejection, like saying, "You're not like the other girls. You're not any fun." As months passed the words returned and settled on me like distilled truth. And as years passed the words began to glow like the highest accolade, words delivered by a young man who somehow saw beyond fraternities and sororities and cheerleaders and football heroes and popularity. That summer night in Ann Arbor, Michigan, a young man named John peered through the window to my soul and told me who I was.

Yerushalayim Shel Zahav

I remained who I was until the age of twenty when my fathomless inner life exploded like a Jackson Pollock painting onto the canvas of the world. At twenty I sailed away on a small Israeli German reparations ship called the "SS Israel" to *Ye ru-shala-yim shel za-hav*—Jerusalem of gold—where I could reinvent myself and where the 50s could not hunt me down. In the holy city, lying with men was how I learned to talk to boys.

In Jerusalem I could be a true bohemian. My nascent adolescent rebel shot like a hot geyser out of the deep, with nothing and nobody to slow it down. Having parents who were liberals—my father was a Marxist in his youth—it didn't seem that outrageous for me to fall in love with an Israeli Arab. I wasn't going to marry him, after all. His name was Toofik, and he was sweet, virginal, and golden as the grapes he brought on our first date. It was an easy love, uncomplicated as Disney. Did I mention he was built like a god?

He took me to a Bedouin wedding in the desert of B'eer Sheva. I sat with the women in the tent as they adorned the bride. To the sensuous music of the oud, the men and women moved around each other in teasing, swaying circles—a ritual wedding dance. The Bedouin women put a black robe on me and pulled me into the circle. My hips moving under the heavy folds of the robe, I danced, knowing I was having the single most exotic moment of my life.

Toofik hoped that I would stay with him, to mix bread with his womenfolk in the sunny kitchen of their house on the Jordanian border, to learn Arabic and have fat golden babies. I had a panic attack one day and bought a plane ticket home. I was no Zionist. I was seeking adventure, preferably exotic, and I left poor Toofik behind as the collateral damage of my year of liberation and debauchery.

I returned home to the house on Drummond Road and landed in a record-cold winter that buried me flake by snowy flake, as I sat in my room with the knotty-pine walls and wrote—a broken, displaced bohemian, a tragic poet with the pseudonym "The Jerusalem Ghost."

So while the hippies were dancing in the streets of San Francisco busy with drugs and free love, I was back in my childhood home, busy with my own private existential crisis.

The Jewish Princess and The Boy With The Monkey Face

Back in Toledo, I met Marc Van Doren, a medieval scholar who lived in a musty flat above his aunt's real estate office. Hundreds of books were tucked lovingly onto shelves held up by Buckeye beer cans. The floor sagged under their weight. That he was a head type was apparent by his sardonic wit and his favorite word "ergo."

Marc turned out to be the four-year-old boy with the monkey face from Breldway Nursery School, the boy I told every day that I wasn't coming back. That was my first lesson in destiny and the cosmic web of connections.

His face was boyish, hopeful, hiding nothing. But behind my face loomed a phantom Jewish American Princess who winced at his threadbare Goodwill overcoat sagging off his shoulders, his incessant smoking, his yellowed teeth, his hacking cough, the name Van Doren.

He wanted us to marry. For him it was that simple. But I choked. It wasn't just my Jewishness. It was his slow suicide death with cigarettes. It was the desperate way he needed me, the way he couldn't drive, the hole in his pants at the symphony the night I wore my mother's seal coat.

The next fall I was studying art history at Toledo U. and he wanted to take me for a church tour of Toledo to show me Gothic arches and vaulted naves— a lesson on the architecture of early Christianity. The mystery of the small glowing candles at the end of long aisles, the women with scarved heads kneeling in prayer—the life-sized Jesus on a cross. I was an entranced visitor from another planet.

He took me to a favorite church on LaGrange St. It was an old red and brown brick Presbyterian church, a friendlier, warmer church. We sat in the back without speaking. Then Marc had an idea. "Why don't we pretend we're getting married. There's no one here."

Like two kids age five, we walked hand-in-hand down the long isle. At the pulpit he removed his high school ring and slipped it onto my finger, and we kissed.

Like a wayward teenager, I would sneak home from the sour-smelling sheets of his shabby apartment at 4:00 in the morning. My poor parents: I, pretending they didn't know; they, knowing everything and pretending not to know. And poor Marc, having to put up with my struggle to remain loyal to my suburban conformist Jewish idea of who I should be. I became an expert at giving mixed messages. In Jerusalem I had been daring, radical—a "free spirit." In Toledo, I didn't know how to just do what I wanted without the fear of hurting everyone in the whole world.

White Raven - 1995
Dear Marc,

As I sit here in this cafe writing my past, I want to tell you that I have bought wardrobes of clothes from Goodwill for me and my kids, and I am appalled that I ever wore a seal coat anywhere. I am no princess. I am Earth Woman. I am an evolved hippie. I am humble. I am no longer young.

As I sit here in the aroma of fresh-brewed coffee, new-age music in the air, I wonder: Did you smoke yourself to death? Or are you a tenured professor of medieval history somewhere back east, with a shock of white hair falling over your eye? And do you drive a car yet? Have you seen the great cathedrals of Europe? Do you have prospects of ever getting west of Chicago?

And most of all I wonder—were we really married in Toledo on that sweet, cold-gray day in the LaGrange Street Presbyterian Church?

Only God knows. I will leave it up to Her.

The Fall From Grace

When I was ten, my mother taught me the elements of knitting. I got good at looping the yarn over the left needle, ducking the right needle under, picking up the last stitch, looping and lifting until I reached the end of the row. I was knitting something yellow, turquoise and pink, the colors alternating every three rows. I didn't know what it was meant to be. It just kept getting longer and longer. If someone asked me what it was, I would say, "It's my knitting." It was something that grew and changed shape every day; it changed shape because of the sides being uneven due to mistakes and gaps where stitches were dropped.

I was walking down the sidewalk on a clear autumn day with my knitting trailing behind me, when a line of bicycles in the street came moving fast toward me. One rider was shouting something to the others. In seconds the line of bikes came up a driveway and one by one they stopped, making a circle around me, the front wheels pointing at me. They were older boys—taunting, jeering, laughing. They wouldn't let me out of the circle.

I stood there bashful, scared, looking down, not speaking, and finally they turned their bikes and left, wheeling and laughing down the street. That was the first time in my life that I had felt real danger.

One day, looking at my knitting dragging two yards across the floor, I felt sick of it. I took it out in the backyard, dug a hole and buried it there. There was sadness in that knitting. It collected sadness and bad thoughts and feelings of not being good enough, and of danger. I buried the sadness, the unevenness, the lost stitches, the taunting and jeering of the older boys. I buried it in the yard.

I was a woman raped. Twice. In two very different ways. When I was twenty-five it happened. Then again at twenty-six.

I had left Marc and moved to Chicago, the go-to place when girls from Toledo left home. I found a seventy-dollar flat in an Italian neighborhood next to White Sox Park and finished my B.A. in French at Roosevelt University in the downtown Loop. I took my last exam on a snowstorm day that paralyzed the city. The elevated trains, the buses, the street cars were still. The city was a trapped animal in waiting. I was right at home in the hard, frozen winter. In my fur hat and high boots I walked home, five miles through the silent virgin snow. This endless expanse of undisturbed whiteness felt natural to me, like something from another time. It was my Russian blood.

I met a man named Allen Goldman, a good Jewish man studying for his Ph.D. in psychology at Urbana, Illinois. We saw each other only when he was in Chicago visiting his family. We were not in love. We thought we should be—a nice Jewish match that would have pleased our parents. He was one of four brothers, and invited me to dinner once at his home. His father sat at the head of the table flanked by two brothers on either side. They all sat there grunting and belching their way through dinner while his thin, sickly mother and I brought dishes in and carried them away. There was no spark between Allen and me. In order to get turned on, he had to sit in bed reading sex stories.

Instead of deciding to marry Allen, I decided to have a nose job. Just a minor alteration—a cartilage scraping would do it—to erase the last vestige of my shy and self-conscious self. In high school, my friends were always urging me to get a nose job. It was going around at that time—as common as braces. For Jewish girls it was practically a rite of passage. But I didn't want the stigma of a nose job.

Chicago was my most beautiful year, and you can only be twenty-five and beautiful once. My face was sweet and inviting. My eyes were gray-blue and I had a perfect rosebud mouth. My chin was soft yet firm. My neck was long and regal. The nose really didn't fit at all. This was not about remodeling my face. It was not about 'show and tell.' No one would even notice. This was a private matter—about the nose inside.

The surgeon came swirling into the room in his starched white coat, glowing white hair—a small man, neat and tidy and impeccably groomed, a cold devil of a man disguised as a famous doctor. When I suggested to him that I had heard of cartilage scraping, he bristled; his face grew dark and angry. That renowned sculptor of women, arrogant misogynist, was hell-bent on revising my face, breaking bones and all.

I was shrinking into the chair and the small man in white was looming larger, all the while talking in a quiet controlled tone about my face, as if he knew my face, as if he knew me. You see, what I really imagined would happen was for him to walk into the room, a kind avuncular man, cup my face in his hand and say, "But, my dear, you have such a beautiful face. You don't need to do this. So tell me, child, what it is you want." But this was not a Woody Allen movie, and this doctor was not in the business of turning patients away.

I think that sitting in that chair when he pronounced sentence on my face was the exact pivotal moment in life when I gave into blind submission, every molecule of me knowing better.

For years I thought of how different my life would have been if I had looked him in the arrogant eye and said, "If you think yourself such an 'artiste,' then get some clay and sculpt some women. This is *my* face and take a last look. You will never, never see it again!" But, being who I was then—a quiet, unassertive, woman—and having shrunk so small into the chair, I shut up, shut down, and thought to myself, *Well, he is famous. He must be good.*

Allen was home in Chicago on school break. I told him of my coming operation. If he had said, "No, you look great the way you are," maybe I would have fallen in love at that moment and married this nice Jewish man. That is what happened to Aunt Rose. When she told Uncle Marvin that she wanted to change her nose, he said, "You are beautiful. Don't change one hair. Don't ever talk about it again." But Allen agreed it would be a good idea.

I returned to Toledo to await the day of surgery. I slept in my childhood bed in the room with the slanted knotty-pine walls. The night before I left for Chicago, my mother stopped me in the hallway. "Are you sure, Laurie? Are you sure?" and she cupped her hand under my chin and brushed my cheek so sweetly with her thumb and said, "You are my doll face."

I went under the knife, wincing at the brutal shock of the hammer blow that cracked my nose, heard loud the scraping inside my skull amid the crescendo of my silent screams. Felt the inside of my mouth being pulled and twisted and sewn. I was under, in a spinning grey vortex—could not move a finger.

Drifts of conversation floating around me. Banter of the doctor and his aids. His golf game, his schedule, and once in a while he would stop the scraping and say, "Look at that. What do you think?" And finally once the bandages were in place, I got wheeled away into my room. There was a girl in the next bed throwing up. She had a small bandage at the tip of her nose, and she and her mother were packing to go home. It seems she had had a minor procedure—a cartilage scraping.

I was staying at my friend Maxine's house post-surgery. It was a party house. There were always people. Allen had returned that week from Urbana. He sat next to me on Maxine's stuffed sofa and he looked into my bandaged face and proposed. Just like that! Right then and there! We had never discussed marriage. We'd never even made a vow of love. I guess he wanted to stake his claim in case I turned out like Sophia

Loren. He proposed to me and then he left, and that is the last time I saw his face, and that is how he remembers mine.

On the day of the unveiling, the doctor, curt and rude, unwound the bandages, gave me a mirror, and I began to die right there in that chair. My eyes had bags under them and my nose was frozen into an awful baboon shape, and my mouth was stiff and abandoned.

I took the long slow ride on the elevated, back to Maxine's house. I felt like a freak sitting there, knowing how I was supposed to look, but no one else seemed to notice. I was just a woman on the train. I never wanted blood and broken bones and bandages and the months of recovery before your skin shrinks back to normal. I never wanted the stigma of a nose job. I never wanted this.

There is more than one way to rape a woman. That doctor was a closet woman-hater, a narcissistic, famous, legally-certified rapist of women, and looming in my mind was the inescapable fact that I had let him.Why this quest for ultimate beauty, for perfection? It went all wrong. This was a crossing over to the dark side—submissiveness to a strange man who didn't even like me, who wasn't even nice—when my instincts knew better. It was as if I had been gripped by a spell—a dark Enchantment.

My most beautiful year was shattered, fragmented like a broken mirror. You go along in life adding layers of charm and *savoir faire.* You learn to give an interview, learn to finesse a conversation with a man you've just met, learn to walk with confidence across a restaurant floor, and then something happens that triggers a reversion to the shy child—all those layers burned away, and you are, in one instant, shrunken and as hidden away as a high school wallflower.

Back in my childhood knotty-pine bedroom, I woke up every day wanting to be dead. My Laurie Me. I searched for her in the mirror and tried to imagine what she would have looked like on that day, what she would have been doing on such a morning.

Mirror, mirror on the wall
where in the world
was she now

Buried

I climbed the steps to Marc's apartment and in my desperation, asked if he would have me back. "I wish you hadn't done it," he said, "but you are still beautiful." And then he looked deep into himself and said, "Now that you are feeling suicidal, you are choosing me over death. Give it some time. You will come back to yourself. I will always be here." He walked out of the room into the kitchen, and I trailed quietly down the stairs, climbed into my father's car and was gone..

Now life was a shape-shifter, with furtive goals and bad dreams. Life was a numbing limbo, and when you are loosened from the ballast of yourself, stray elements can come flinging in as if from the devil's own sling shot. Once you pierce the comfort zone, in come the dark forces, like murky waters through a broken dam.

At twenty-six, I completed my teaching degree in French at Toledo University—back on track, yet with a persistent sense of doom. One day I got a call that a school in Lorain, Ohio needed a French teacher for winter and spring quarters. Lorain was a dismal industrial city, suburb to Cleveland. The president of the PTA, Mrs. Martin, offered me the house of her aunt and uncle who were out of the country.

I taught French to fifth and sixth graders. In the school's punishment-based system, the smart-ass kids would collect demerits all day, and at the closing bell the ones who had "earned" the most demerits were lined up against the walls of the hallways, bent over, hands spread against the wall, and the teachers would go down the line with a paddle. It was a backward school; yet they taught French to fifth and sixth graders! *Miséricorde! Mon Dieu!*

I lived in that house by myself and counted the days until summer. Mrs. Martin's aunt and uncle were Catholics, and there was a four-foot statue of the Virgin in front of the fireplace and in the bedroom, large crucifixes on the walls. I turned the Virgin to face the wall and removed the crucifix that was over my bed.

The other teachers sat in the teachers lounge and smoked. I never talked to them. Every day after school I returned to the house to correct papers. Every weekend I drove home to Toledo. Once in a blinding snowstorm, I spun around three times on the freeway, but I drove to Toledo no matter what.

One warm day I returned to the house, a stack of papers to grade, in a jolly mood. Only two more weeks of school before summer vacation would release these smoldering, restless children into the sizzling Lorain summer. In the evening, I put on a Dionne Warwick record, the one where she sings "Alfie" and "What the World Needs Now is Love, Sweet Love." I cranked it up and danced sexy around the living room. I ran a bath and sank into the water.

Sounds in the kitchen. Rattling of silverware in the drawer. Hallway lights snapped off. Footsteps coming close. I froze and called out, "Who is there?" No answer. I scrambled out of the tub, wrapped a towel around me. *Got to get out of here. . . this is the end . . like the Richard Speck massacre of nurses . . .I have nothing on. . . no lock on the door. . . this is how I will die.*

The bathroom door was thrown open, the light switched off. He grabbed me from behind and said, "I'm going to kill you." Alcohol on his breath. He told me to shut up, threw me down on the living room couch, pressed a spoon against my throat. He felt my breasts, called me babe, said that I was asking for it. He struggled with his limp erection, blamed me for that. He bolted out the door, cursing, dropped the spoon in the front yard, ran to his car, and drove off.

When the police came we sat in the kitchen, two officers facing me—my eyes smeared with mascara, my hair a mess. I told them what I could remember: he was white, short hair, medium height, drunk—that he drove off in a light blue sedan. I didn't know the make. They told me to come to the station the next day.

They left. I turned on all the lights. I sat up in the bedroom all night waiting for the sun. When morning came, I got dressed, took my papers, drove to the school. The teachers had read about a rape in the paper. They didn't know I was the one, or if they did, no one said anything.

Mrs. Martin, horrified at learning what had happened, drove me to the police station after school. They insisted on speaking to me alone. The two male officers sat across from me at a large desk and began the grilling. "Is this anybody who might have seen you in a bar, anybody you might have talked to in a local tavern?"

"I don't go to bars. I never go anywhere except school and my house."

"It sounds like someone who knew the house, someone who had been watching you. Is there any way you might have given him a reason to follow you?"

"I never saw him before. I never go anywhere in Lorain. I go to Toledo on weekends."

"Where did he touch you? What did he say when he touched you? Show me the marks on your neck from the spoon."

They wanted to believe, they wanted me to believe, that I had somehow made this happen—that I was asking for it. They wanted a hot story. They wanted a cheap thrill. They wanted details, dirty words. They wanted signs of struggle. They wanted more. I walked out of that room raped again, knowing that this young sick man would never be found, knowing that this report would be filed away and forgotten—wondering what I had done to make this happen.

Mrs. Martin and I went to her aunt and uncle's house to clean it before their arrival home. We scrubbed the floor as if to exorcise the devil. She turned the statue of the Virgin back around, and I wondered privately if I had hexed the house when I turned it to the wall.

It wasn't until I was home for the summer that I told my parents what had happened. They had no words for this. They could not speak of it. They were making plans for a second honeymoon in St. Thomas via Puerto Rico and, not knowing what else to do for me, asked me to come along for the first part of the trip.

At age twenty-six I sat in Puerto Rican restaurants with my mom and dad, sipping rum drinks. I lay on warm beaches in the Caribbean sun. My face got burnt and the skin around my nose became deeply creased. I was ugly and maimed and ruined.

The last night before my parents left for St. Thomas, we went to a nightclub. Dionne Warwick was the guest star. Standing tall and beautiful in a slim white dress, she sang "Alfie" and "What the World Needs Now is Love, Sweet Love"—American sailors swarming the stage around her feet.

'Buried,' whispers The White Raven. I buried those rapes, as do many women. I buried them as I had once buried my sad knitting in the ground. I went on with my life. No therapy. No returning to it. It was just a bad bump in the road—nothing to do with my real life. With my mythic childhood at my core, I thought I was okay.

I escaped all those mishaps of the Midwest.

I moved to California.

PART 2

The San Francisco of our Love

"The heart has its reasons,
which reason knows not."

- Blaise Pascal

CHAPTER 1

Starving in the City of Love

White Raven,

When the glory days of Greek civilization were over and the dancing Muses abandoned Mt. Olympus, they blew with the winds to every cranny and crevice of the world. Free Spirits now, they wander the Earth; they come when called—as they have always come.

The Muse has always been real for me—her presence, as well as her absence. What better way to explain the flash of a poem in the shower, or words sneaking into my head while driving so that I have to pull over and scribble them down before they are lost. The Wandering Muse has also abandoned me for years at a time—just adios! No goodbye kiss on the cheek, no forwarding address.

Toledo, 1968

THE NIGHTS WERE SO LONG and slow and heavy you could not bear even the touch of a sheet. A hot swampy Toledo summer with air so wet you could drink it.

It was dusk, and I was sprawled, half-dead, in a lawn chair in the backyard of the house on Drummond Road. I, who have thick Russian blood and lack the sweat glands necessary to cool a body, was slowly suffocating; I rolled over and fell in a heap, the smell of damp lawn in my face, thinking, *This would be a good time to be somewhere else.*

I was a "been-abroadnik," a BTI (been to Israel). I had escaped the repressive 50s and had lived a bohemian life in Jerusalem. My high school friends back home who had found their lawyers and doctors in their freshman year of college were married and talked of baby things. At age twenty-six I was back in Toledo again, wondering if I had really left at all. Every time I set sail to explore the world it was as if I were auditioning for a life, and if things got rough out there I would return to the green oasis of home, to my perfect mythic childhood.

The late 60s was a time of fomenting, and I was fermenting in Toledo where the counterculture was a B movie with a bad script written by my people, a gaggle of misfit intellectuals, conscientious objectors with guns, and college dropouts. I took part in Civil Rights in a Toledo sort of way. On a midnight escapade, a fellow radical and I dumped a can of white paint over a black jockey lawn ornament in the rich neighborhood of Ottawa Hills.

I was the only white person in CORE (Congress of Racial Equality), sent out to apply for jobs that my black friends would then apply for, to test for racial discrimination. I was mortified the day that the group met at my house and we all filed past our black help, standing at the ironing board ironing my father's shirts.

One Friday evening I went to the temple to hear a student from California lecturing on Jewish Renewal and the New Age. He proclaimed: "There is a revolution going on in the streets of San Francisco. Flower power, hippies dancing to conga drums, high on life. Rabbi Shlomo Carlbach is the spiritual leader of Jewish Renewal. He writes music and plays guitar and young Jews flock to the House of Love and Prayer in Haight-Ashbury and go crazy with dancing."

I listened in an altered state—the speaker might as well have been an alien with a greenish glow coming to abduct me—and then he said "The Summer of Love," words exploding through me like a hot shower of fireworks. In the temple of Toledo, the God of Israel was whispering to me personally:

> "Something is happening out there and you are missing it. Go to this far-away place from which you cannot so easily return home. And may your Childhood finally rest in peace."

The red rooster weathervane on top of the house on Drummond Road was pointing in one direction—West.

In fall of 1968, I packed a typewriter, art supplies, books, records and my Midwest clothes into my new blue Mustang and sped west as if my life depended on it—through Omaha, Cheyenne, the great salt plains, and on and on through the night.

Almost one hundred years ago on her immigrant voyage to this country, my Russian Grandma Fanya stood at the ship's rail reciting in her most elegant English, Emma Lazarus's poem: "From her beacon hand glows world-wide welcome. . ." waiting for Lady Liberty to appear in the New York mist—when the ship pulled instead into Baltimore! A poignant moment lost to history. But when I crossed the San Francisco Bay Bridge in the haze of early morning, the radio was singing like an anthem, like a hymn: "If you're going to San Francisco, be sure to wear some flowers in your hair." I checked into "The Hotel California" and there was no going back.

Grandma Fanya and I both looked west to find a new life. She is gone now, but she comes to me in California dreams, still traveling west.

When I left Toledo that final time I closed the curtain on the tree-arched streets and castle houses, and landed in a cockroachy room in an old residence hall (something Arms) on Bush Street in downtown San Francisco. I came west with one check from Toledo that I couldn't cash anywhere. Well, that's almost true. My father was president of People's Watch Repair with leased departments all over the country. I knew I could take my check to any Macy's or Sears watch repair and be saved, but I wanted the anonymity of independence—and I nearly starved.

I wandered from bank to bank and not one would cash my check. Hungry and desperate, I sat at the desk of an officer at Wells Fargo and told him I hadn't eaten in three days, which was the truth. He looked into my innocent blue eyes, pulled a twenty out of his pocket, and handed it to me. I broke my fast at a café, trying nonchalantly to sip a coffee and pick at a sweet roll—to be one of the working people having my morning brew.

In truth, I was almost too late for the 60s. I had already missed Jerry Garcia playing free concerts in the Haight. I'd missed Mario Savio's passionate Free Speech Movement for the multitudes at Berkeley. I had missed the Human Be-In. I had never had an acid trip. How could I tune in and drop out when I had only just dropped in? An immigrant from Toledo, I was doing what immigrants do: looking for a job and a place to live—and the only way I knew to look for a job was to get all dressed up in a coordinated outfit and take typing tests.

In a suit and black patent heels, I walked up the steps of Sproul Hall at UC Berkeley weaving in and out among the college hippies sitting like yogis and chanting to the sun. Everyone. Everyone. *I want to be like them*, I said to myself. My soul had driven me to San Francisco, but sometimes your very soul has to loosen up before it can 'be-in.'

When I was eleven, I went to Hebrew School and I was a good student. My old-world teacher, Mr. Smullen, soft-spoken and gentle, one day sat down next to me and said: "A person has to have a name. Call yourself a Hebrew scholar. Give yourself a name."

Abandoning Toledo in 1968, I had vowed that in my new California life I would finally be an artist—give myself a name. I had a fresh raw talent, but I'd taken a wrong turn years before, got derailed and drifted from one job to another as a typist with good English skills. That was what I had to sell, and in those days it could get you in anywhere. I signed up with Kelly Girls, worked jobs in the San Francisco financial district, walking among the best-dressed women in the western world.

But the Wandering Muse was watching. She had followed me, hitched a ride to California. She had grown up since she first came to me in the closet at Breldway—had blossomed into a tall hippie in a long gauzy dress and gold hoop earrings. She took me by the hand and pulled me to every seedy downtown life drawing group in the city.

I had the right stuff. My artist uncle had told me so. My room was soon full of drawings taped to every wall. I set up an easel in the kitchen. I kept busy. And I was as lonely as I had ever been, working temp jobs in the west's most romantic city—unknown, invisible as a bug, uncared for by any living soul in the entire Bay Area. I cried myself to sleep at night.

"Soon," whispered the beautiful Muse who had a slight buzz-on. "You will have a better place to work. Soon."

Actually, there was one person in the Bay Area who knew me—my old high school friend Sandra who lived in a Victorian in Haight-Ashbury, and was waiting for the war in Viet Nam to be over so her husband could return from his tour as a troop psychiatrist. Sandra invited me to a party in Berkeley.

CHAPTER 2

When A Wallflower Eats A Magic Brownie

WE WERE NOT A MATCH. That Berkeley night when I met Tom Corn might have been the last time I ever saw him. I entered the smoky, candle-lit apartment dressed in a green fitted coat, under that a brown jumper with black turtleneck shirt, and under that black tights and a black panty girdle down to my knees. I looked for my usual spot in a corner by the wall where I could disappear into the smoke and watch the party. But as everyone was sitting in a sort of circle on the floor, I sank down in the nearest vacant spot, stealing glances at the lanky man in the purple psychedelic paisley sweater sitting next to me.

He sat lotus-style, rocking slightly to the beat of "Keep on Chugglin." He had a pale boyish face with heavy horn-rimmed glasses and light brown curls sitting high on his head. His feet were long and delicate, bound in thin-strapped sandals, and I couldn't help staring at his toes with digits as long and flexible as fingers. Although he looked nerdy, his eyes were busy following the hostess whose legs stemmed audaciously from a black leather skirt cut just below the butt.

The air was fragrant as joints were passed. I had had no experience with pot except one time in Toledo (where it was called a narcotic) when a friend and I had sat on the roof of my suburban house smoking the joint her lesbian lover had sent from New York. I had sat in my bedroom in terror, waiting for my stony state to be over so I could go downstairs to dinner.

There was a plate of pot brownies that was slowly disappearing. I ate a large one, and the entire world changed after that. Forever.

"What do you do?" I asked the man in the purple sweater.

"Try and guess," he answered with an edge.

"Student?" I offered.

"Nope. I'm a metallurgical engineer at Lockheed."

I launched hopefully into a book report on *Worlds in Collision,* the pseudo-scientific account of how all the world myths of flood and famine were based on the near collision of Venus and Earth. The purple sweater was cringing, but I went right on with my book report, and his eyes went right on chasing the leggy hostess around the room. This would have been a good time to move to the other side of the room, but I was more a wallflower than a social butterfly. I would have lost my place on the floor, and I would have had to start all over somewhere else.

So I changed the subject. "Where do you come from?"

"Southgate, near L.A., but I spent all my summers in Toledo with my grandfather." Finally, an icebreaker that could melt ice.

You were not a match? interjects The White Raven. Who says that we are not sometimes drawn to danger and discord? A woman attracted to a man who is not paying attention to her, so she does not give up trying to get his attention? Is this unheard of?

"Let's get out of the house," he suggested. "Just a walk around the block." He rolled a joint. I buttoned my green fitted coat and we descended the long flight of steps leading from the back door to the yard below. I was really stoned by then. As we rounded the block I clasped my hands behind my back and walked, looking down.

"I just discovered why my grandfather Sam was always looking down when he walked. It's because he had his hands behind his back like this." Great marijuana revelation. He rattled on about this and that, and suddenly I couldn't recall his name. "Don't tell me." I said. "Let me think of it." But he blurted out "Tom."

"Why did you do that? I would've remembered. You didn't listen. You talk too much." It was the brownie speaking. He stopped in his tracks.

"No one ever said that to me before."

The spreading trees of Berkeley glowed peachy-yellow in the streetlights. It was breezy and the limbs waved us on as we walked. The air was cool, mysterious as Halloween. We came back around the block to where we had started, although I could have been anywhere on the face of the earth and a year could have passed, so stoned was I. When we reached the yard of the party house, he walked behind me up the steps and in an unconscious reflex, his hands shot out and landed on my hips just for a second. "What's this? A panty girdle? Get rid of it." At the top he kissed me, a small confident kiss, and in that moment something happened—something warm, unexpected, and strangely familiar.

"Can I call you?" he asked.

"If you can remember my last name," I teased, "you will find it in the phone book."

"What is it?"

"Perlmutter."

He called the next day and every day after that, for many moons to come.

I am a romantic. I so wanted to star in a story of love at first sight. When I was little I used to ask my mother: "Tell me again, how did you and Daddy meet?" and in her sing-song voice she would say: "I was sitting on top of a green hill and he came riding by on a white horse." How could she know I'd believe it all those years?

They dated awhile and then my father backed off. She waited day after day knowing he was the one, until she had waited long enough. She dressed herself carefully, rode a bus to downtown Toledo, sauntered swingingly into his office and stood there. He looked up, was startled, then amazed—and in that moment six children became a part of destiny. I wanted to star in a movie like that.

White Raven,
What nudged me to eat the brownie, walk with him around the block? The bad signs were all there: his reluctance to talk to me, the wallflower; his disdain for my book report; his eyes following the hostess around the room; his comment about my underwear (the nerve!). But signs are just signs. They are not law, like a red stop sign, like the descending gate at the train crossing. We just chug right on through the bad signs as through a turnstile, following uncertainty and the unknown as if they are beacons in the night.

There is alchemy when two souls connect, and where did this soul connection begin? Was it Toledo. . .that elemental world of normalcy, a world ordained with rainbows, the precious seasons turning and turning?

Not a match—yet, our first encounter held the patterns, the tone, even the script of what was to come. That night in Berkeley, all the ingredients were brewing, bubbling. You could almost smell the brew. Pot, sex, loosening up, other women, jealousy, walking together, shyness, fantasy woman, insecurity—all there.

Maybe he didn't want to like me, and maybe my instincts were telling me to be careful, but our souls were paying attention as we walked around that block. And in this soul connection was the beginning of a long and tumultuous story with bewitching love leading it on, and incipient danger in the brew.

CHAPTER 3

Trying on California

"Do I love you because you're beautiful
or are you beautiful because I love you?"

- FROM THE MUSICAL "*CINDERELLA*"

WE TOOK A TRIP TO Yosemite. In Tom Corn's red VW bug, we climbed Sierra roads, snowflakes flashing psychedelic patterns as they rushed like a light show into the windshield. We rented a tiny cabin and played in the snow. We had packed light—a change of clothes, a jacket, gloves—and as we left home I had grabbed the paper bag of pot from the counter.

Now in the warm cabin, ready for a night of pleasure, Tom sat on the bed, opened the bag to roll a joint, and yelled, "Oh no! What's this?" pulling out a chicken bone, some food scraps, and a butter wrapper.

"Oh-oh. I grabbed the wrong bag," I murmured.

"I guess I'll have to get used to this," he said, softening, and we made amazing love, as if to seal the fact that we belonged together in some cockeyed way.

It was the sex. Always the sex. He looked like a nerd; he was a lover. The first time we made love, it was fun, orgasmic, surprising. He didn't look like he would be that kind of a lover, but he had just broken up with a woman he'd made love to every day for three years and had plenty of practice and plenty of drive. Over the months I continued to be surprised until the surprise turned to expectation, and the expectation to hungry need. I was fuck-struck, hooked and landed.

Some men are endowed with enough "yin" that tuning into a woman and knowing how to please her is as natural as rain in Brazil. Tom was well endowed (with yin and otherwise) and besides, he was an ultra sensualist. He loved quality food, great music, pot, and sensational sex. Yin, yang, hung. He had it all.

My school teacher clothes were tucked away in drawers. I was finally loosening up, trying on California. My skirts got shorter. My pants got flowier. If we hadn't taken a walk around the block that night in Berkeley, it is likely that I would have managed to wriggle out of my panty girdle and go native. But with this man it was happening fast, and I liked what I saw in the mirror of his eyes. And through my eyes he was transforming too. When I drew him—and I drew him often—what appeared on the paper was a man more solid, more masculine, older, with the shadow of a beard he didn't yet have.

CHAPTER 4

Portrero Hill

You lived on Portrero Hill
near Army Street
in a dark basement pad
with cement pillars
a low ceiling
green and red square melmac dishes
piled high in the sink

I would come to visit every night
and sit shyly
on the edge of the bed
until you said "Take off your coat"
You had to tell me every time
It was always a first date

And then in that bed
between the Bozak Concert Grands
speakers as large as refrigerators
such passion raged,
such womanscreaming passion
I lived for it
I nearly died each time

"You must not, ever, give anyone else the responsibility for your life."

-Mary Oliver

Tom's flat on San Francisco's Portrero Hill was in the middle of the low-income housing projects. He chose that hill for the radio reception. He was a connoisseur of classical music. In his UC Berkeley days he went to the music lab every day to explore something new. Although his mother was a piano teacher and at one time a promising concert pianist, Tom never learned to play an instrument. He fancied himself more a conductor. When he listened to music stoned, his forehead began to churn and he could conduct an entire symphony with his eyebrows. Tom loved that I was musical too. I grew up with the classics, played Chopin on the piano, and I strummed guitar and sang folk songs with a pretty Joan Baez voice.

Soon after I met him, he bought two giant Bozak Concert Grands that flanked his bed, speakers as large as refrigerators. I had never heard sound like that. Maybe it was the pot. Maybe it was the loving. Maybe it was the 60s. The music that blew from those Bozaks was non-directional; the whole room vibrated. It wasn't loud. It was big, and like big sex, we couldn't get enough of it.

I was drawing again, and writing poetry too. The Muse when She likes you and you have set Her free, is fusion of air and fire, earth and water. She is wild and fierce, fluid and deep. And she doesn't have limits and she doesn't have a name. The Muse ravaged me like a storm, and love was the spark.

When a woman is brought to peak ecstasy by a lover, she is at risk of becoming a love slave. It happened to me. He was in charge of where we would eat, what music we would listen to, what I would wear. I didn't care. He was the boss of me. Never had I been so pleasured—over and over and over, each time different—each time an epiphany and a healing.

Despite all that ecstasy and the seeming fact that we belonged together, Tom made it clear that the San Francisco apartment was his place. I found this out when I left a blue polka dot dress hanging in his closet overnight. "We don't live together." he said. "The one thing I'm most afraid of is anyone being dependent on me. When I see your things in my closet I get nervous." So my clothes and my things lived in my apartment in Oakland. And he unfailingly called me at work every day saying a casual "Howdy. Want to come to dinner?" and there was never a question of where I would be spending the night.

I met Tom's mother in San Francisco. She took to me immediately since we were both Toledo girls and we both played piano. When I mentioned that my father played violin, she asked me who had been his teacher in Toledo.

"He had a French name," I answered. "He was my father's teacher because his studio was upstairs from my grandfather's watch repair shop in downtown Toledo."

"Really! Was the name Peret? Jean Peret?"

"Yes. That's it. Peret."

"Jean Peret was Tom's real grandfather! And he was your father's violin teacher? I don't believe it!"

"Then how is Tom's name Corn?"

"Well, that's a long story—a sort of skeleton in the closet story. Peret was an eccentric musician and a lady's man. One of his pupils was a talented pianist named Helen. He fathered her child and she later married a man named Corn. I always told Tom he could have had the name Peret if he chose to, but he always preferred Corn."

"I don't relate to the French name." Tom chimed in. "Doesn't feel like me. Corn is a good American name. But I relate to the music."

Destiny was orchestrating this—violins and all.

CHAPTER 5

Bikini

I WORKED A $400-A-MONTH JOB in the offices of Dymo labelmakers adjoining the factory stinking with gigantic rolls of embossing plastic. There I met Susan who was beautiful and ample-bodied and blond, with stunning blue eyes and a hint of British accent picked up from her English parents. She was a professional by day working her way up in Dymo, and by night an adorable funny blond who smoked reefer and talked stony. She had a boyfriend, Bill. They would soon marry.

We were planning a trip to the Russian River on the weekend with Susan and Bill. I pulled my blue bathing suit out of the drawer and Tom recoiled. "You're not going to wear that, are you?"

"Why not?"

"It's one-piece. This is California. You'd be ridiculous. Everybody here wears a bikini. You'd look like a hick from the Midwest. Besides, with your body, you'd look great in a bikini. Loosen up."

It was the "loosen up" challenge again. "I don't know. I look best in simple one-piece suits. I'm just not the bikini type."

"If you wear that, I'm not going to the Russian River with you, not in that thing!"

So the next day after work, we were in the locked dressing room at upscale I Magnins, he sitting on the floor, me testing a pile of bikinis. I had a flashback to the days when my mother would sit in the dressing room with me as I tried on tailored navy blue dresses, I deferring to her good taste because I didn't have any of my own.

The one we picked was a two-piece suit of orange and tangerine floral design showing plenty of cleavage and belly. We went to the Russian River. I was proud and sexy and full of myself.

But it was never enough. Tom was obsessed with how I presented myself. He wanted my Toledo to Go Away. He had just finished ten weeks of encounter group marathons and Bioenergetics therapy to learn to be closer to people.

"I think you should go to one," he said. "You could use some help learning to express yourself. I'll pay for it."

The marathon weekend was held at the home of an artsy woman in her forties, in the foothills of Mt. Diablo. We sat in a circle on the floor, and the leader, Ben Printz, a tall, curly, dark-haired man, laid down the rules. No phone calls. No leaving except for emergencies. He had an eager and aggressive manner and seemed to love being the center of attention. Just as well. I did not want to be noticed.

We were directed to have a short conversation with the person sitting next to us and then write them an uncensored message on our perception of them. I unfolded the paper given to me by the man sitting at my side and read, "I don't find you an attractive woman. You are not feminine enough for my taste." In his world, did feminine mean having painted finger and toenails? Batting your eyelashes? Cleavage? Being petite and flirty? Was he too young to know the difference between feminine and womanly? In reading his note I was altogether flattened, devastated, ruined. It is decades since then, and I have not forgotten the sting of those words.

We went around the circle telling why we were there. I volunteered that I was there to watch, to see what happens—that I wasn't exactly sure why I was there. There was a loud and collective reaction. They were not interested in having a voyeur in their midst. They formed a circle, holding hands, and I had to break through. I got down on my hands and knees trying to crawl in under the circle of joined hands, creeping like a dog from person to person. I would have preferred a quiet morning at home with the Sunday paper. But I pretended to care and finally, they let me make it through. I stood in the center of the circle. They crowded close and hugged me. I was in.

These people were experienced encounter group junkies. I was green, vulnerable, and alone. Married couples entered the ring, Ben Printz egging them on into conflict, forcing confrontation. They cried, swore, beat each other with pillows and ended up reduced to a loving heap on the floor amidst a gallery of cheers.

In the middle of the day Ben decided it was time for some real feelings to surface. He lit a joint and it began its way around the circle. I had never smoked serious pot except with Tom, and even with Tom I sometimes became paranoid. Marijuana, for me, could be the sweetest aphrodisiac, or it could augment feelings of isolation or craziness. I never knew which way it would go.

I took a deep breath and held it so long that I got stoned beyond the zone of safety. I didn't trust these people. I liked Ben least of all. He was attention-grabbing, rude and crude and without warmth. Warmth? Irrelevant in this crucible of raw and uncensored feelings. I stole into the bedroom and found a phone and called Tom. "Please," I pleaded. "I'm so stoned. I hate it here. I want to come home. Please come and get me."

Helen, the owner of the house, burst into the room and shouted, "What do you think you're doing? You're putting me and all of us at risk talking on my phone about drugs! You're not supposed to be making phone calls. What's wrong with you?" she shrieked. She left the room and I stood in tears. *None of this matters,* I thought. *I will never see these people again. I just need to make it through.*

I wandered back into the living room. It was lunchtime and there was light rock music on. Some of the women had stripped down to their underwear and were dancing around the room. There was nothing in this scene that was in the least familiar or comforting. Nothing. But maybe that was the point.

I filled my plate with spaghetti, drifted out into the backyard and sat alone under a tree. People settled in small groups eating, talking. Up in the tree was Ben. He was squatting in his underwear on a branch chimp-like, beating his hairy chest and making monkey noises, bouncing the branch up and down. He jumped down from the tree and began a Shakespearean soliloquy.

I came up behind him and said, "You are the most verbose person I have ever met," and dumped my plate of spaghetti onto his head. Never in my life had I done such a thing. It was the pot. I was expressing myself. Maybe I did need attention. Maybe I was doing my work.

The world stopped. Everyone stared. In spite of the ominous silence, I returned to the kitchen feeling that I had finally done something worthy. Suddenly from behind a hand grabbed me around the middle and something warm and wet and soft was smashed into my face. I was sure it was excrement, then realized it was mashed potatoes. I turned, and Ben was sauntering away, looking satisfied with himself.

When the group reassembled, I announced that I wanted to leave, to go home. They all agreed that what was needed here was a healing. They had me lie on the floor and approached me one by one, throwing arms and legs all over me—a smothering mountain of bodies, a human pile of love.

I escaped on the second day with no plan of returning. My friend Susan from work and her boyfriend Bill were getting married in Oakland. Tom and I barely talked in the car. In the church I felt disoriented. The wedding was out of a Fellini movie. I saw the future of their marriage, their problems spread like tea leaves in a cup. Bill was possessive and Susan was smashingly beautiful. I knew they would not last. I could not pretend.

In the weeks to come, I could not stop being angry. Tom was puzzled. "Whatever happened at the marathon, you have learned to express yourself." I was so disturbed that I decided we should separate. I remembered who I was before I turned into a love slave. Aphrodite needed a vacation.

"I have to leave you, Tom. I have to go back to Toledo for awhile. I can't be your fantasy woman all the time. I like my one-piece bathing suit. I *like* who I was before." He looked stricken. He couldn't think of anything to say. He didn't try to stop me.

I went to work the next day and Susan saw me crying at my desk.

"What's going on?"

"Oh, I don't know. I think we're breaking up. I mean, I told him we were, but I don't know. Anyway, I'm going to Toledo in a few days. I'll know better when I get back. Tom just doesn't accept me the way I am."

"But he loves you. I know he does. We'll see. We'll see."

Susan dropped me at the airport and as I was walking to the gate, a tall lanky, curly-headed figure was drifting toward me like a mirage. "What are you doing here? How did you know my flight?"

"Susan told me. I wanted to see you before you flew away. I'm going to the mountains to think, going backpacking by myself. I'm leaving today after work. Can I meet you at the plane when you get back?"

"Yes." I promised—tentatively.

CHAPTER 6

The Zone

Lockheed

There is a morning cock that wakens me
It rises before dawn
drawing the sheet up around it
nodding up and down

You get up
aim it toward the closet
and follow it there yawning

You zip it, bulging, into your pants
throw on a shirt
and kiss me slowly
deeply
goodbye

I DON'T KNOW WHAT GOD revealed to him on the mountain, but when I returned from Toledo he picked me up at the airport and wasted no time saying that he wanted to live together. "I found out what is important to me. I want to be with you." I caved. He said those words out loud: "I want to be with you," And once again, I was hooked and landed.

We rented a Spanish stucco house in San Francisco. We would walk hand-in-hand to the small Italian restaurant down Monterey Avenue and eat mushroom and sausage spaghetti. Next door to that was the King of Hearts ice cream parlor where we would stand hand-in-hand like two kids, trying to decide on a flavor. There was a mom and pop store down the street owned by an old German couple.

For furniture, we made pillows. Together, we picked out fabric: a golden pattern in satin, a turquoise and white paisley, and for our love bed, a green fake-fur full-size pillow. I sewed while he mixed the stuffing. He discovered the best mix was half kapok (cotton) and half shredded rubber. We poured the mix, choking on kapok dust, into the pillowcases.

In the evening we would take walks through St. Francis Woods—richly landscaped Spanish houses rising up out of the hilly streets adjoining our neighborhood. We never walked anywhere without holding hands. Our hands would join like magnets. It was a physical fact—like gravity, like osmosis.

We were smugly self-contained in the orbit of our little world. There were only three people invited in: Susan and Bill, the newlyweds, came over on weekends. We would smoke a joint and feast and dance, and in the morning they would be in a heap where they had landed the night before.

The third visitor was Michael Luckie, Tom's gay friend from his Berkeley college days. Luckie was slender, slightly stooped, with thinning brown hair, a prominent beaked nose and receding chin. He had an engaging laugh and a Woody Allen charm. Mike loved classical music as did Tom, and their repartee included such debates as whether Mozart's "Symphony Concertante" was serious classical or lightweight.

Luckie was not depressive, but definitely self-deprecating. He frequented the bathhouses of San Francisco when the unknown AIDS virus was in secret ferment. He once confided in me that he didn't expect to see old age, didn't want to, really. "Once a gay man loses his looks, he has nothing going for him."

I had a new job at the Bureau of Jewish Education, working mornings as secretary to my rabbi boss, and crossing the Golden Gate every afternoon to teach Hebrew to a bunch of unruly pre-teens in San Rafael who were putting in the required hours to earn their Bar or Bat Mitzvah. They were literally jumping out of the windows and running around on the second floor roof of the temple. I was terrible at discipline.

Tom continued his commute to Lockheed every day. He rose before dawn, threw on pants and a shirt and was gone. He worked the SCAN electron microscope, analyzing photos of metal fractures on the Agena Missile and writing exquisite reports.

At the day's end when I pulled into our street and saw his VW bug parked in front of the house, the secretary-teacher parked her blue Mustang and out of the car emerged Superwoman, hungry and insatiable.

We lived between the giant Bozak speakers flanking the fireplace on the Technicolor red shag rug. We had dinner between the speakers. Breakfast. Lunch. We had each other.

Between the speakers was the
Zone Called Paradise.

In the early days of our love Destiny was celebrating us with violins, oboes and flutes. A walk hand-in-hand to the ice cream parlor, and sweet harmonies poured from the clouds. But now, Destiny brought in the whole ninety-piece orchestra: crashing symbols, sweet bonging bells, cheerful chimes, pounding pianos, victorious violins, triumphant trumpets, heavenly harps, and a caroling chorus of "Ode to Joie," conducted by Aphrodite herself.

Music profound. The deep madness of music. He absorbed it like no one I'd ever seen. He imbibed it, swam in it, he had to have it. Every kind of music: Mozart and Mendelsohn, Bach and Berg, Brahms and Julian Bream and Villa Lobos, Thelonius Monk and Coltrane and Miles Davis, and on weekends The Rolling Stones and The Beatles. I was full of the music, full of love, full of him. There could not have been more. It was perfection. Whatever crevasses we would someday fall into were not yet even hairline cracks. Toledo was drifting farther and farther away. I pulled in my sails and I was Home.

Some evenings the stage was set with candlelight and the music of India—ragas with sitar and drums vibrating low and slow between the speakers, then quickening and rising in intensity until the vibrations themselves were having sex: tika-tika-ta-ta. Ta-ta-tika-tika-ta. A man and woman held by the gathering waves of the drums, as they rocked and swayed on the green love pillow, and at the climax of the drums the woman would catch her shadow on the wall, arms waving like a cowgirl on a bronco, head thrown back, and she would wonder who she was and where she'd been all her life—while the ghost of a wallflower from Toledo sat fading once and for all into the wall, and the jangling hippie Muse, much amused, danced willowy and tall around the room.

and will you remember the candlelit
marijuana nights
my spinning shadow on the walls
crazy with dance
mirror, mirror on the wall
who is the wildest of them all
look at me, look at me now

my hips are holding you, a gentle vise
you are weight free in the air
let me carry you
it is no trouble
I want to
take you for a ride

Ta-ka ta-ta tik ta-ka-ta. . .

CHAPTER 7
Hippie Wedding

"If I get married, I want to be very married."

- Audrey Hepburn

Tom had plans. He had once driven through the mountains of Montana and had vowed to return someday to walk the trails of Glacier Park. On my birthday he took me out and bought me a pair of tough, high-topped Swiss hiking boots. In the weeks to come we bought backpacks, ropes, a *bluet* stove, tube tent, Sierra cups and a pot. He already had the double-mummy red sleeping bag, big enough for loving, big enough for two.

The engineer began to do what he did best: to plan, research, design a perfect hike during his two-week vacation slot at Lockheed. We spent all our weekends in Berkeley at the Ski Hut—Tom studying contour maps, I picking out khaki pants with deep pockets, hiking socks, and freeze-dried food packets such as "just-add-water" chicken tetrazzini, and powdered eggs and cheese.

Then Montana began to rise inside our living room. He enlarged a contour map of the trails, cut it into squares, and attached them to adhesive-backed cardboard—and then with a utility knife he carved out each contour and glued them one on top of the next, mountains and valleys appearing like magic. Every evening after work he would sit on the floor cross-legged at the redwood round table, and carve and dream. In the end, we had a six-by-six-foot relief map of the portion of Glacier Park we planned to hike.

I had never slept outside in my life. Not even in a tent in the back yard. Not even in Girl Scouts where a camp-out meant cooking baked beans on a grill in Ottawa Park. And I was no athlete. Athletic endurance for me was riding my blue Schwinn bike around the flat neighborhood of Old Orchard. But I have Russian blood and I am strong and I have stamina. And I was in love.

In July we flew to Great Falls, Montana, and from there, rode the minibus to the Park, past the Sleeping Giant Mountain, through Native American territory. When we arrived at Glacier, the trails planned down to the last hour of the last day, we stopped at the ranger station where the ranger told us that the trails of our itinerary were closed. "Still snowed in. You'll have to make alternate plans," said he.

Tom's face grew ominous. All that planning, all that carving wiped away by a simple "Snowed in. Make alternate plans?" So we set off anyway, I with blind faith in The Man—and the passes were passable and we slid down snowfields like the grizzlies at play, alone in a snowy world under big Montana skies.

Lovers alone in the wilderness will never be the same. There the love between a man and a woman can bloom and swell in an Adam and Eve sort of way. We left a trail of love through those snowy mountains and were walkers together from that time on.

Tom's vision was for us to hike Glacier year after year, each time on different trails. I had a vision of my own somewhere along the way: a man and woman hiking, and behind them, three or four little hiklings trailing after in miniature boots, holding little walking sticks. I was almost thirty and I wanted ducklings.

He was scared, scared shit. Scared of the end of other women, the end of the looking—the beginning of responsibility. This was the 60s: for him, a time to let go, expand, smoke weed, party, play, love—not to retract, settle back, marry and have kids. I wanted all that good stuff too, but I wanted to lasso it, pull it in, hold it tight so it wouldn't get away. I too was a pack rat for pleasure, but I was from Toledo, almost thirty, and I wanted ducklings.

I wanted to marry him. Actually, it was more that I wanted him to want to marry me, but he couldn't say the words and my wanting became enormous. Once he said to me, "There's something I want to buy for you, but you have to come with me." Naturally, I thought "ring" although he didn't seem like the engagement ring type. So he drove into downtown San Francisco, parked the VW bug, grabbed my hand and turned into a music shop. "I want to buy you a guitar. You have to pick it out."

I concealed my disappointment, secretly dubbed it "my engagement guitar," and continued my appeal. "I'm almost thirty. I want to be a mother, and for that we should be married." He agreed on this condition: "Before the baby, we are going back to Glacier."

We had a hippie wedding in the living room of our Spanish stucco house. Dick York, minister of the Berkeley Free Church (an iconic figure in the documentaries of the 60s) with his big Afro hair and long white robe, married us. It was a haphazard affair; we had given only two weeks' notice. Susan and Bill were there and Michael Luckie arrived in a trim white bell-bottom suit. Tom's parents, two of my siblings, and Mom and Dad, were the only family.

Mom and I made tuna fish hors d'oeuvres in the kitchen. I wore a long satin dress of many colors. My rabbi boss had given me a fancy menorah for a wedding gift that stood like a benediction on the mantle between the two vases of flowers that my father had bought. We sat on our love pillows on the Technicolor red shag rug. I borrowed my mother's wedding ring. And from the wedding vows that I wrote for us:

Let us plant the seed of Corn
that he may grow tall and straight into the universe
and by him, learn to change
and through him, change the world
Let me make you feel warmer when you are cold
Let me make you feel younger when you are old
Our language is love
Our language is love

Once the wedding guests had departed we dove into our big green stuffed pillow bed and just before making love, Tom said thoughtfully, but fully out loud: “If I were to ever see Ann LeBeau again (the woman he loved before me), I don't know what I would do.”

The day after the wedding, we went to Golden Gate Park and Tom suddenly climbed a tree. I'd never seen him climb a tree before, but he picked a tall one and disappeared like a squirrel straight up that tree, out of sight into the foliage, while I stood there looking up, thinking: *What is he doing, making a widow of me on my first day of married life?*

White Raven,
Tom Corn was a researcher, a scientist, a planner. Yet, when he took that solo trek to the mountains and returned imbued with the desire to live with me, that was an emotion-based decision—something he badly wanted. This marriage thing was different. He felt pushed. The hippie-dippy wedding vows I wrote were my own projections of what should be important. It's almost as if his agreement to marry and get pregnant was a trade-off for my agreeing to return to Glacier.

CHAPTER 8

Planting The Seed of Corn

To stay true to our plan, Tom, in research mode again, calculated the conception so that we would be just five months pregnant at the end of the hike in Glacier. Any more than five, and the backpack hip belt would be too tight. And I who was the sexy and perfectly receptive vehicle for this plan, got pregnant at the precisely calculated time.

Every generation of teens thinks that it discovered pizza. In the 70s we acted as if we had discovered massage. I recall that Marin weekend in a stony, dream-like way.

Jeffrey Conner and Alice Kelly, well-known massage practitioners, were holding a weekend workshop in a lavishly rustic home in the Marin hills. There were people of various ages—some couples, mostly singles. We could wear clothes or not, as we wished. Most of them walked around in underwear.

Jeffrey Conner was a fox. He took us through the various techniques, and often he would choose me for a demonstration, insisting that this was not sensual massage, not meant to arouse, all the while running his hands up and down my legs with just the lightest stroke of the upper thigh.

By the time evening was upon us I was Hungry Woman. Tom and I stole out to the backyard and made crazy love in the double-mummy red down bag. I remember the rest of the workshop through a shower of pixie dust. Colorful carrot raisin salads, pastas, creamy soups, a line of women in their underwear dancing to light rock—I feeling quite special, knowing somehow intuitively, that I was with child.

In the coming months, as I was growing a baby in my belly, Tom was busy reading Rodale's bible on organic gardening. He wanted to grow things too. We got permission from our landlady to plant a vegetable garden behind our Spanish stucco house. Tom dug up the backyard. He built a greenhouse and covered it with plastic. For pest control, he imported jars of ladybugs and Praying Mantises that arrived in the U.S. mail, bought red netting at a fabric shop to keep the snails out. Project man was on—a man possessed.

He drove to a farm up north of San Francisco where he got free hay for mulch, filled his VW bug to the roof with warm, composting hay, loaded a U-haul trailer with more hay, and drove home. Picture a VW bug pulling a U-haul full of hay getting stuck in San Francisco on the busy corner of 19th and Sloat, and be glad you weren't there.

Tom Corn was a driven man. I believed in Him; like a religion, I believed. It was clear that there would be no mediocrity, ever; that there would always be projects; that every project would be a mad adventure; that no two days would ever be the same.

And the vegetables grew—like the famous Scottish Findhorn Garden where a spiritual community collaborated with nature spirits. The vegetables grew—and for the first time I, who had shunned the slimy canned vegetables of Breldway Nursery School, learned the true taste and texture of broccoli and spinach, leeks, and even kale.

It was a foggy summer day. I was six months pregnant, out for a stroll through the vegetable garden. I remember what I was wearing—maternity jeans and the light purple sweater that Mom had knitted. I accidentally stepped on a small plant on the border of the garden. He yelled, "Watch out!" Then he gave me a tour of the greenhouse cabbages, the onions, tomatoes, carrots. On my way back to the house, somehow I managed to step on that plant again. His hand shot out and he slapped my face. I sat down on the ground, stunned and quiet. I had never been hit—maybe one disciplinary spanking as a child—but never by an angry hand. And I was pregnant. And it was a plant.

I want to believe that later he apologized, but can't quite remember.

CHAPTER 9

The Green Monster

Eve sat anxiously in the Garden awaiting Adam.
Finally, late in the night he returned to his vexed
and agitated lady.
Eve: "Where have you been? Is it another woman?
Adam: "But Eve, you are the only woman in the Garden,
. . .yay, in the whole world."
"Come closer," she implored, "Let me count your ribs!"

IT IS AS OLD AS man and woman. It is not right, wrong, good or bad. It is biological. It is only in looking back that I can see why for so many years that green monster jealousy sat on my shoulder like a gargoyle. Why at every party I watched him like a hawk, like a territorial fox, like a hurt little girl. For so many years.

In the days between the speakers, there wasn't much that pushed through the "no trespassing" sphere of the Zone called Paradise—until one summer night. There was a knock on the door. A curly-headed woman named Karen introduced herself as the daughter of friends of my Grandmother Perlmutter. She was a fresh refugee from Buffalo. She was comfortable, fun, easy to like. The three of us smoked pot, and when she was in the shower Tom and I sneaked in and we all soaped each other up.

Karen settled in Mill Valley, fell in with a crowd of boat people from Sausalito, smoked pot and loved dropping acid and taking walks on the ocean. "The ocean," she proclaimed, "is the only thing you can depend on."

She had a hallmark laugh. She quaked with laughter, and once when we were in a Mill Valley restaurant she went on a laughing jag that set off the whole crowd, staff and all. In the months to come she went native. She lost weight, her short thick hair became long black bouncy ringlets, she dressed hippie, sewing her own clothes, and once when she visited us, she got stoned, stripped to her underwear, and began to do yoga with uncontrived and innocent grace and beauty. I watched Tom's eyes watching her.

One day I heard him in the bathroom on the phone. He was joking and laughing in a low, secretive voice.

"Why were you in the bathroom talking on the phone?" I later asked.

"Because you are always watching me. I just don't want to be watched all the time. I was having a conversation."

That day a tiny worm-like errant thought wriggled into my brain, formed itself into a question mark, hung there in the gray matter—a small voice asking, *"Am I enough for you? Are you **still** looking?"* From that day on She was in my life.

The Other Woman

A phantom seductress: her hair is black. Her hair is red. Curly. Long. Short. She is tall and willowy. She is stocky and brown-skinned. She is funny, sultry, shy, vivacious. She is inside of him. Inside of me. She is Everywoman. Everywhere. Always there, observing. Waiting in the wings. Outside the Zone. Watching for her cue.

Tom could not ignore a smile from a female stranger. It was a green light that he had to follow. Marriage for him was the end of actual physical relations with other women, but relational possibilities thrived and became enormous. Because he wasn't running around having affairs, he thought of himself as innocent, and in a conventional way he was. But his fixation with Other Women was excessive, and something he liked to share with lucky me.

In the beginning I found this intriguing. So, he was a lover of women; that's a good thing. He had his favorite body types—usually tzavtik *(hefty)* or women who dressed to be looked at. I looked at them too. I could have gone into a room with two hundred women and told you exactly which ones he would be attracted to. In those early days, in the San Francisco of our love, if we were driving and I spotted one of these women, I would invite him to go around the block so he could get a better look. What was I thinking?

CHAPTER 10

Papa Daddy Tom

I want to walk big with child
to have men offer me a seat on the bus
When I am six months, my belly just begins to swell
At seven months people admire how well
I carry my baby, at how I barely show
and I just want to be Great with Child
Where is the ripe melon of my belly,
the classical nude belly of the photo exhibit?

My babe rides safe
within the confines of my ever ample hips
I carry him deep and low and safe
within the bony temple of my hips

You can plan a conception—we had proven that—but the rest is a matter of the stars, of learned expectations, of common sense or the lack of it. My parents made it look easy raising six. I thought that if you just fed and watered them, they would grow up healthy and happy. "Zei gazundt," (Be healthy) as Grandma Fanya used to say.

There are hundreds of books on how to raise children: books of names, stages of development, trends in conscious parenting—but not so many on how to survive as a couple. But this I know. No matter what a man gives to his wife, now the Mother, it is not enough. It can never be enough. She needs it all: the inviolable bond of Mother and Child and she needs support, moral and physical from The Man. And in the end, the Mother is still the Woman. Still the Woman.

I went by myself to the first La Maze class, and came home dreary because the whole room was full of couples, the men sitting on the floor with their mates. Throughout the following weeks of class I'm sure everyone was thinking I was a single mom. Tom surprised them, showing up at the last session as the instructor explained the stage of labor called transition when the woman might want to hurl something at her coach. It must have been at that moment that Tom decided he would be busy taking pictures. He was a master photographer, and he shined up his lenses and checked his light meter.

Tom knew, when it came to birthing and woman things, that anyone who conceived the way I did and who danced rock n' roll with a baby-full belly, did not need pampering. He did his part in driving home the seed. He had no doubt that I would be superstar of the maternity ward. In other words, he did not fuss over me.

Four months pregnant, we were visiting friends in Stockton before our Montana hike, and they were curious about backpacking pregnant. Tom dispelled their concern with a cavalier: "Well, even if we lose this one there's more where that came from." Tom Corn had a way with words. A pregnant woman already knows her baby, and he is not just the result of some random spurt of semen.

At the UC Med Clinic I never saw the same doctor twice. They all had different opinions about backpacking. One told me it was fine, but "Don't be too far from a phone!" Then, finally, a young doctor gave his blessing: "Just use common sense. Don't carry too much weight. Don't climb rocks. Your center of gravity is always changing."

We hiked. I was proud, vigorous, and the baby inside got plenty of mountain air, rain, snowy meadow, and Montana sky. No wonder he grew up always trying to get to the highest place out in the middle of nowhere.

On December 9th, the alarm clock next to our bed did not go off. I looked over and nudged him: "Tom, you'll be late for work."

"Work! I'm not going in today. This is your due date!" I guess he thought that on the due date some blue lights would go off and the show would begin. Two weeks went by. I took long walks. I danced. At the clinic one intern (whom I had never seen before) swung into the room, looked down at me in the stirrups, and asked, "Why isn't your baby here?" Sheepishly, I looked up at him, as if I had done something wrong. He stuck his fist up me (or so it seemed) and loosened the membranes.

That night after we returned from Boris and Mary's Russian restaurant, I began to have cramps. I called the hospital and reported: "I'm having cramps, like menstrual cramps. Is that anything to worry about?"

"You're in labor," said the voice in the phone. "Contractions feel like menstrual cramps, only bigger." Hours later deep in transition, my face contorted with the pain of back labor, the doctor (another one I had never seen) popped in to tell me I had a long way to go. My body knew better, and within minutes I was in the birthing room being slit from hole to hole (by another doctor I had never seen), and the baby came beating the air with his world-free wings, his father in a green hospital coat having photographed him in his flight to planet Earth.

When they brought him to me I looked into that sweet round face and called him Benjamin. Tom wasn't ready to agree, so the hospital named him Baby Corn, and for a month we called him Pookie Face.

It was the week before Christmas. The sparkling Christmas tree at the end of the corridor lent a sad sentimentality to the maternity ward. The day after the birth I lay in bed in tears. A big kind nurse came to me and said, "Oh honey, it's just your hormones. It's the post-partum blues." I talked birth and labor with the other women on the ward. I wrote a poem. My milk came in like hot burning coals. The baby learned to nurse. All seemed well.

Then, on the day we left the hospital and drove across town, all the security vanished out the window; suddenly I was responsible for this little life. I was terrified.

It was shortly before Baby Corn's birth that Herzog came to live with us. He was a friend of Michael Luckie. Herzog was in his sixties and homeless. He walked with a limp, wore old worn-out clothes, plastered the long strands of his thinning hair sideways over his balding scalp, and wore a tweed cap all day. He was an ex-teacher, an intellectual with sardonic humor and witty observations on life that he pulled on cue from his faithful cap.

When his marriage ended he fell apart and attached himself to his friend Mike Luckie. Tom and I offered him one of the unused bedrooms in the back—just until the baby arrived. Herzog was a natural cook. He could stay with us, in exchange for cooking and running small errands. All he required was a room and a steady supply of cheap beer. His only other requirement was that I stay out of "his" kitchen.

"You will never be a homemaker," he chided. "You are always leaving the cupboard doors open, and you can't pick out a good tomato." We would shop together, he showing me how to pick out a good tomato: "firm but no soft spots." And later in "his" kitchen he would metamorphose apples, a cut of roast, potatoes, carrots, and turnips into a gourmet feast. I was willing to expand on Paradise a little to let Herzog stay.

I trusted him. He was harmless. He respected me, spoiled me, flattered me. I think now that he loved me. I don't really know what Tom felt about all this because he didn't say much, but he couldn't argue with the meals at night, and Herzog had promised to be gone when the baby arrived.

He wasn't. On the evening that Tom and I drove home with Baby Corn, Herzog was there at the door to greet us. From that day on he called Tom "Pappa Daddy Tom," and tried his best to remain indispensable. The meals became even tastier. The house was immaculate.

Herzog had a friend named Chris, a dropout from UC Berkeley. When Chris came over they would have all-day scrabble tournaments. The board would fill up with fifteen-letter words I had never heard of. I would sit in the room nursing the baby. They would preface this occurrence with: "Here come the beauties. Here comes the flesh!"

One day Herzog and I drove to downtown San Francisco for a baby item I needed. I left Herzog in the car with Baby Corn while I went into the shop. Minutes later, he wandered into the store.

"You left the baby in the car, alone?" I ran out, relieved to find him there asleep in the baby seat. "You never leave a baby alone in the city. He could have been kidnapped!"

"Ah yes. Tut. Tut. There are kidnappers lurking around every corner waiting to capture your baby." I failed to see the humor in this. Something shifted in that moment. Herzog knew his time had come, and in a week he was gone.

So was my solid gold custom wedding ring made by a local artisan. I kept it on the mantle, as it was too loose and needed sizing. I searched pawnshops for a while, but never saw it again. Wedding ring. . . gone.

My mother came to visit. She came, as all mothers have come for centuries, to pass the baton, guide me in the ways of motherhood—bathing Ben in a plastic tub on the dining room table, turning him this way and that. The first evening of her visit, Tom arrived from work and sat outside on the front steps waiting for this mothering extravaganza to be over and for dinner to materialize.

That moment—Tom sitting out on the step—was the beginning of the end of the Zone Called Paradise. One day I discovered that the small room downstairs in the garage had become his secret man cave complete with girlie magazines tucked under a small sofa. The uni-sphere of our love was split, and he and I began spinning in separate orbits—Mother and Babe in one, and he, the displaced Love of my Life, off on his own trajectory.

On Sundays we went to Hippie Hill in Golden Gate Park where children ran around and women danced to the conga drums in soft clothing and no underwear. Whatever progress I had made in loosening up was lost as I skidded backward into the familiar and straight world of mothering as modeled by the truest mother of them all—my own moonfaced mother. At Hippie Hill I felt like an anomaly—a boring den-mother wife. I sat and watched as he moved around the circle of dancers, capturing the hippie girls with the long lens of his Nikon F.

I complained that he never took pictures of me. He explained: "It's just different. It couldn't be natural or candid. You're self-conscious. It would look posed." That didn't help any.

If he smiled at a waitress in a restaurant I couldn't sleep at night. If he exchanged words with a low-bodiced bawdy woman at the Renaissance Pleasure Faire, I felt my world crashing. I began to hate The Other Women, hate the camera—and the errant worm, the tiny question mark embedded in my brain, was growing fat and hungry, asking over and over if I would ever be enough for him whose eyes were forever roving, wandering, wanting more than I could ever be.

> *This man, my husband, had "anima lust" explains the erudite White Raven. "Anima," in Jungian psychology, is the archetypal woman within the man, connecting a man to his unconscious. If anima becomes an obsession, the man may become a Don Juan compulsively engaging in sexual or fantasy adventures.*

But here's the thing: the man afflicted with anima lust has to be able to relate to, even to revere, other women while being savvy enough not to sabotage his relationship to Number One. That is where common sense, tact, and maturity come in.

CHAPTER 11

Bad Boy

The conga drums are beating
stony dancing on the green
A long-lens camera
juts from your middle
a phallus
aimed at the braless hippie chicks
click click
One dances for you,
hips rocking, arms
undulating like underwater seaweed
you follow her in circles
click click
while I sit
holy and forsaken
Madonna with Child
on Hippie Hill
my milk turning sour
with the hate

BILLY MACK LIVED IN THE house whose backyard was adjacent to ours. He came over one day and introduced himself. He was a garage mechanic. He had on overalls, had unruly black hair, intense bright eyes, had the look of the bad boy—fast, slick, smart. He was curious about us—about me.

He began to show up when Tom was away at work. Bad boy became my confidante. He saw clearly that my displaced anger at Tom was focused on the hated camera; he got ideas. I talked. He listened, commiserating with me, asking how Tom could resist taking pictures of me when I was so attractive. He was working me, coming on strong, and I was just a little bit into him and glad that something was happening to balance Tom's flirtation habit.

We had a darkroom in the downstairs garage. I had learned to develop pictures, and whenever Ben was sleeping I would hurry down there to unroll negatives and develop photos. One day Billy Mack followed me down to the darkroom and we began to make out. We were hot. This bad boy made me feel beautiful and naughty. It was hard to stop, but I did. He backed off, but he knew he had me.

One day he came with a proposition. He said I could get back at Tom for his camera escapades and make some money too. He would take the camera, hide it at his place, and I would report it stolen. I recoiled, doubted I could pull off such a thing. But I did. I called the police and reported the theft. Then I called the insurance company. They sent out an investigator. I declared the value of the camera with all the lenses and attachments. We had no prior claims; nothing was suspected.

Tom was devastated. He couldn't believe someone would come in and steal just the camera. I was sick with guilt. How could I have lied to him or taken a chance like that? Did Tom's flirtations turn me into someone *that* unhinged? A mad woman? A maenad? What was happening to me? I wished for Herzog again. He kept me laughing. He was safe. He was a miserable man, but true to the core.

In a few weeks the money came. Billy and I split it down the middle.

Later, bad boy returned the camera and I told Tom what we had done. He got very quiet, had to absorb this new information about his wife. We never spoke of this incident again.

"Hell hath no fury like a woman scorned," quotes The White Raven. Old Shakespeare knew what he was talking about. How I struggled in deciding whether to include this story—goody-two-shoes me. Larceny, fraud; this was a part of me I had not met before. This was like an episode in "Desperate Housewives."

Was it my desire to please Billy Mack that drove me forward with this scheme? My finally having a way to fire a warning at Tom? My attraction to the bad boy and my shadow? Billy Mack was Hermes, the divine trickster. He may have been into me, but mostly, he was an opportunist, a con artist.

And maybe Bad Boy was just what I needed—just what the doctor ordered.

CHAPTER 12

The Hill on China Grade

TOM'S LOVE OF GARDENING HAD flared into a burning desire to move to the country and grow things. Maybe the name Corn really held an unconscioius draw to farming, something so strong it pulled him from our neat life in the City of Love through the redwood forest, into the country, onto the land—with visions of terraced orchards and goats and maybe even a pond with fish—a place where everything was possible. And I was destined to follow, because what else could I do against so strong an ancestral pull?

I was scared. Tom and I were not close, and I clung to what had been so good: the music, the loving, the mama and papa store, the Italian restaurant down the street. Moving to the country sent fearful shivers through me, waves of foreboding. But as always, I gave in to The Man, let him lead the way as if he were Moses leading the troops through the desert.

We took long drives all over the coast, once to La Honda off of Pacific Route One, the woodsy community where the Grateful Dead, in a backwoods cabin, had practiced their music. One day at work, a co-worker of Tom's mentioned Boulder Creek, a small town in the Santa Cruz Mountains. Land was cheap and it was commuting distance to Lockheed Missiles and Space.

From above, our VW was a tiny ladybug on a mission, winding through an immense woodland of green. I sat in the passenger seat, head turned to the window secretly crying, as our faded Campbells-soup red beetle twisted its way up the Highway 9 corridor, every mile driving us deeper into the primeval forest and farther from our home in the City of Love.

My mind kept snapping like a magnet back to the living room of our Spanish stucco house, hazy with pearly smoke of the blessed drugs, the red shag rug in the Zone between the speakers where love had bloomed and swelled. Swallowing tears, I asked myself why we humans try to improve on Paradise. I turned to look at Ben, now almost a year, his sweet round face floating in dreams.

Tom had come to accept my passive, non-assertive manner, and I was charmed by his perfectionist ways and his over-zealous drive. He had supreme confidence in himself, and I did too, because apparently he could do anything. I turned to watch his hands on the wheel. Strong hands, yet tender and knowing.

In my four years out west I had transformed from middle-class Jewish girl to Bay Area hippie. And now I was about to evolve (devolve?) again, to join the migration to the mountains. Folks unplugging from the city, squatting on a parcel of land—back-to-the-land earth people. Married couples barely survive kitchen remodels, and our marriage was fragile enough without subjecting it to the building of a house in a mountain town light years from the mapped world.

The car climbed the switchbacks as if it knew where it was going, the engine whirring, as VWs do, like a wind-up toy. I wished it would break down. Maybe Tom would see it as a sign that we should turn back, and we would change our minds about buying land in the boonies and go back home. Eventually the road leveled out as we passed The Mountain Store and coasted into the funky little town of Boulder Creek, nestled like some lost civilization in the heart of the Santa Cruz Mountains. We walked around the three-block town with storefronts and signs of the old west, one reading "Mac's 100 Year Old Place." Jack's General Store was the main shop, stocked with flannel shirts, wool socks, mud boots, and raincoats.

"It rains about sixty inches here, so I'm told. I guess we're in for a mean winter," offered Tom with an inflection I hadn't heard before.

"Already you sound like a local," I chided.

"Don't panic," his standard reply whenever he, himself, was ill at ease.

Next to Joe's Bar was Al's Lemon Chicken where we went for lunch. It was like the bar scene in Star Wars: country rock music, rednecks planted on counter stools as if they'd been sitting there for all time—locals who knew each other, talking loudly across the room. It was too smoky, too noisy, too close, and I stared into my plate. I had always been good at going native, blending in. In my year in Jerusalem I had learned to walk Israeli, speak street Hebrew without an accent. Here I felt more like a tourist than I ever had in the Middle East.

Bearded mountain men were standing around outside Joe's bar. They looked me over as I climbed back into the VW and strapped Ben into his seat. Trucks lined the curb, each with a built-in toolbox and a panting Pit Bull in the back. *How could I live here? I have a college degree. Who would I talk to?*

We went to a real estate office and were taken to a parcel of land for sale on China Grade Road, a mile past the Boulder Creek Golf and Country Club. We trudged up a steep hill, three acres of rising wheat grass meadow. Our socks were full of scratchy stickers, but that was forgotten once the view at the top revealed itself. Tom stood there gazing at the magnificent vista of redwood mountains veiled in mist, and at that precise moment of time, his vision became real, spread out right there before him—the terraced gardens, fruit trees, even the pond with fish, and maybe chickens and goats walking around. And I could feel our lives lurching from the safety of The Zone Called Paradise into the forests and winding dirt roads of the mountainous unknown.

The land, the agent said, was once wooded, but after a big fire only stumps remained. The hill became a favorite place for Easter egg hunts, known by the locals as Easter Egg Hill. Tom had brought a shovel and began digging up some samples of dirt, putting them in containers.

"What's that for?" asked the realtor.

"I'm taking it to Lockheed for a soil analysis." The realtor raised his eyebrows.

The soil passed its test—certified organic by Lockheed Missiles and Space. Tom, who had already decided, could hardly wait to revisit the land. My father had agreed to lend the money. Three-and-a-third acres for only fourteen thousand.

On our next trip to the land, we bypassed the realtor, and as we neared the top we saw a woman from the house across the street climbing up the hill.

"Hi! I'm Mandy. I saw you two up here the other day. If y'all are interested in this property I can tell you about it. I make my living in real estate." She was tall, her long legs stemming from blue jeans shorts. Soft brown curls framed her all-American face, and based on the accent, she was obviously from the south.

"This hill was originally owned by ol' Mrs. Crawford who lives down there in that green house across the street. She used to own all these parcels on China Grade. If y'all are really planning on buying this she would want to meet you. In fact she'd probably require it. She's real old, kept alive by a pacemaker, but has definite ideas on what should happen to this land."

"So if she's not the owner how does she have a say in who buys it?" asked Tom.

"Well, years ago she gave the parcels to her sons and daughters in hopes they'd settle in the country and pass on the land to their next of kin. Her son Lionel who owns this hill moved to San Jose. He was no gentleman farmer, b'lieve me. Old Mrs. Crawford cut him out of her will."

Tom laughed his falsetto laugh.

"Well, come on over when you're ready and have a beer. Then we'll go see about ol' Mrs. Crawford."

When we knocked on the door of Mandy's house a tall hulk of a bearded man answered and introduced himself as John, Mandy's husband. He had a deep voice and walked stiffly as if his back were killing him. John was a comfortable kind of guy who gave Tom and me the once over, commenting, "You're city folks, right? Where from?"

"San Francisco. She's from Ohio originally."

"Just some advice if you're moving out here. Time is different in the mountains. Things move slowly. It'll take you a good five years to lose your city. But things'll work better once you do. You smoke weed?"

"Sure," smiled Tom.

John took a glass pipe from his shirt pocket and lit up. "There's a little cabin in a meadow up the road where some guys blow these hash pipes."

Tom drew on the pipe, had a coughing fit, and I had one tiny puff. The room began to spin and I went out the door and sank down on the front lawn where I lay watching the trees dance, feeling panicky and sick. I could hear drifts of music and laughter inside the house. Tom's falsetto laugh. John's deep resonant voice. Tom seemed to fit in despite his "city." Where there was pot he was right at home, and in my head: *I don't want to be here. I hate being stoned. It makes me feel crazy. I'll never fit in.*

Tom came to collect me and I peeled myself off the lawn, went to get Ben who was playing with Mandy's and John's two boys in the backyard. Ben too seemed at home anywhere. Just give him a sandbox and some cars and trucks to push around.

Old Mrs. Crawford sat in her rocker looking over the Corn family. I sat quietly holding Ben, as Tom went on about his plans for terraced orchards and organic gardens. She did not write him in her will, but Mrs. Crawford could die happier now. She gave the green light, and in two days we were in escrow.

> *White Raven,*
> *You have taken away my table by the window and replaced it with a gift display: earrings and cards and hand-made clocks from redwood burl. It is sad. I will fly away, nomadic and free as a raven, wandering and writing in no particular place. But, White Raven, you will still and always be my voice, my Muse.*
>
> *Everything changes. As Karen once said, "The only thing you can depend on is the ocean."*

PART 3

We Quit Paradise and Landed in The 70s

from the Enchanted Land of Childhood of the 40s
into the make-believe bubble of the 50s that burst
into the wind and fire and sweet revelation of the 60s
that spilled out into the backwoods of the
Santa Cruz Mountains in the 70s
when Enchantment once again fell upon the Land. . .

White Raven,
In the 1970s a new species arose on the Pacific coast: land pioneers, homesteaders, ex-professionals who dropped out, bought land cheap, moved into trailers, tepees and shacks, and we became a part of it. We thirty-something hippies came west with our college degrees and abandoned middle-class values and became ganja-growing entrepreneurs. We were "earth people," slightly underground. The marijuana culture bloomed and spread up and down the coast. Small towns became psychic enclaves where people were tuned into each other because everyone was smoking homegrown.

Restless souls from the eastern seaboard sped across the great plains and deserts to places such as San Francisco, Berkeley, and eventually mountain towns like Boulder Creek. The 70s settled on that little logging town nestled in the Santa Cruz mountains—lit it up, softened its redneck core. Buddhist settlements began to "budd" in the backwoods with a new breed of California Buddhist.

Unconventional without pretense, anti-establishment without guile, we were social pioneers (or renegades, depending on your point of view), side-stepping the rules of the monolithic County Building in downtown Santa Cruz. We got reprimanded by the building department authorities from time to time, but there were too many of us living in tepees, half-built houses without codes, trailers without permits. They couldn't just wrap us up and ship us back home to Ohio or the Bronx.

We were not pioneers in the way of our predecessors who came in covered wagons to homestead on the land, but we lived as they did—primitively, with stubborn optimism, and outside of convention. They lived in scarcity because they had no choice; we lived that way on purpose. We lived life raw, we lived it hard, we lived it simple, we lived it third world. We lived it passionately, sufferingly, close to our instincts.

Where did all the flowers go? They migrated out into the small towns, up into the mountains, down winding dirt roads over sacred Native American creeks, into the backwoods. Onto the land. The hippies were not done. They were on retreat.

The 70s was our Avalon—a mystical realm known only to those who entered and lived in accordance with a certain truth and spirit of a time that was outside of time; we had our goddesses, our Merlins, our music, and our magic. Like Avalon, that era has drifted away into the mists, never to return.

So, come with me to the hilltop where I used to sit gazing at the distant ridges of the gently rolling Santa Cruz Mountains, asking myself: How have I landed on the top of this hill with a man named Tom and two small children?

Come with me. There is no rush. In the 70s, time was taking its time.

As you begin your ascent through the blond wheatgrasses, scratchy fox-tails sticking in your socks, you will see the logging road and the hills rising behind the small white house across the way. Keep going, and the first mountains will become visible, tree-studded and deeply green. Keep climbing, and the next ridge of pines and redwoods will appear, a bit more muted in color, and finally you will arrive at the top. You will catch your breath at the panoramic view of the distant layers of mountains, a soft mist drifting through the feather-like redwoods tickling the blue hill-scalloped sky.

CHAPTER 1

Michael Luckie

I DROVE TO DOWNTOWN SAN FRANCISCO with Ben in the back seat sleeping. Sweet Ben, a love, never demanding. He could play for hours with his little cars and trucks, and his smile lit up my world. I was going to visit Mike Luckie who lived with his partner in an old Victorian, to say goodbye.

Mike had been Tom's best friend in his Berkeley days, but they had drifted apart—possibly because Luckie was openly gay and Tom might have found that a threat. Maybe Tom's lack of manly physique made him feel uneasy when they were together. It was Mike and I who had become close friends. I could talk to him. He was my confidante, my girlfriend.

Luckie answered the door of his second floor apartment, bowed and ushered us in with a flourish. Dark, red velvet Wagnerian drapes covered the tall Victorian windows. The furniture was heavy and ornate.

"We're packing, moving in two weeks. I'm going to miss you, Mike."

"I'll miss you terribly. How is it for you, the move?"

"It feels like there's no turning back now. Tom's drafting the house plans himself, you know. He asked me one night to give him a sketch of how I see this house of ours. Well, we used to take walks through St. Francis Woods, looking at houses to get ideas. So one day I made a sketch of a cottage-like Welsh house that I especially liked. It had paned windows, and in front, a low, sloping, rounded roof.

Well, he ran with the idea of rounded sides to maximize the view of the mountains all around, and now it's all his. Out of my hands. He is planning to build a huge mountain home—bigger than the one I grew up in with my five brothers and sisters, and it will sit at the top of a naked hill—sort of like a castle."

"I guess that makes you sort of like a feudal queen then," Mike chuckled.

"Or sort of like a damsel in distress," I moaned. "Everyone, especially Tom's stepdad who is a civil engineer, is trying to talk him into a simpler structure. The roof is complex, and he wants it in pure copper sheeting. But he won't change a spec on the design. He says it's "the whole gestalt that counts."

"And you can't chip away at a gestalt," said Luckie, shaking his head.

"The thing is, our marriage is already fragile. Ever since this little guy was born Tom stopped seeing me as superwoman. Now I'm supermom and his eyes are always wandering. I've never been jealous in my life before Tom, never had reason to be. But with Tom, every time he smiles at a waitress I freak. We go to Hippie Hill and he walks around with that zoom lens undressing all the hippie chics and I sit there feeling like the housemother of Hippie Hill. I just don't get it. And he thinks his flirting is so innocent. It's like he just never got over being a high school loser, so every time any woman gives him a smile he has a compulsive fantasy about her."

"Hello. Did you just notice? He *is* a compulsive. About everything: music, women, gardens, the house. But he loves you, you know. He probably just wasn't ready to be a father."

"Well, ready or not, he is one. You know Tom. Everything in his world is something he researched, something he has control over. The only thing he had control over with a baby was driving home the seed. He was so stoked when he planned our conception to the day. But now that there is a baby, what is he supposed to do with it?"

"That I can relate to. Remember the first time I saw Ben? I looked down at him and he peed a fountain right into my face. I couldn't relate either," he laughed, as I reined in Ben who was in the act of rearranging all the objects on the coffee table.

"But you know, it's this compulsive stuff that makes him so interesting to me," I continued. " He's a nut case and a genius, and I like that. He's a trip." I looked down, my eyes hot with tears. "But, it's true, now that I'm a mom it seems more important to just be normal. I find myself wanting to be more like my mom who had it all—a stable home in a house they built, and my dad giving her everything a mother could want. The truth is I keep wanting Tom to be like my dad. I grew up believing that marriage should be easy. I still believe that."

"Tom can never be your father. His father deserted his mom on the day Tom was born. He never had a happy childhood like you did. Let him be what he is, and maybe he'll grow into his fatherhood."

"He grows into it and I get the growing pains." I looked at my watch. "I've got to go now. I have tons of packing to do." I wrapped Luckie in a warm hug. "Come visit us in the mountains," I whispered, my voice breaking.

"I will. I wouldn't miss it, oh Great Mountain Mama."

CHAPTER 2

Came The Rains

ONE NIGHT AS TOM AND I were packing, Billy Mack brought over a group of itinerant hippies. We got high, turned on the Rolling Stones, and a woman named Andie floated down on our green love pillow. She was thin, graceful, smelled of Patchouli oil, and was clad in a long gauzy skirt and a see-through blouse revealing loose breasts. Her voice had a soft ring and an enchanting English accent. Tom moved over close to her and they talked in low tones.

That night I dreamed of women dancing like nixies around Tom on luminous-green English hills, while I sat in a black dress on the edge of the woods wanting to scream, but unable to make a sound.

A week later as we drove to Boulder Creek, Tom broke the silence with a question. "You know that woman Andie?"

"Yes, I'm aware of her."

"Well she was telling me the other night that she could use work. I was thinking she could come live with us when we move, sort of a nanny for Ben. She could help clean up the house—only for awhile." Then he added, in a slightly combative tone, "But you probably wouldn't care for that idea because I think she's pretty cute."

My heart was racing and a cord tightened in my left temple. I wanted to scream but no words would come out, and I felt a headache clamping down. That night, as I sat blanket-wrapped in a chair immobilized by a migraine, I replayed the scene over and over in my mind:

> *"But you probably wouldn't care for that idea because I think she's pretty cute."*
> *"Stop the car. Let me out of here." I slam the car door, stand with Ben on the edge of redwood forest hitching a ride to town.*

I rewrote that scene all night in bed, forcing him to pay attention to me, forcing him to remember those nights in the Zone Called Paradise when we were the only people in the world.

We moved to Boulder Creek, rented a dark, depressing house that Mandy, our real estate neighbor, located for us in Riverside Grove, a crowded, winding neighborhood of cabins deep in the redwoods. The rent was cheap, probably because the house had been deserted for months, the electricity and gas shut off. Also, there were stories of a murder there. Dope deals and murder. I could feel it.

It was the height of winter and the rains never stopped. The house was dank and dreary and cold. A huge, blackened fireplace was a gaping, medieval hole in the living room wall. The kitchen with a battered old unused refrigerator, broken countertop, and peeling floor, put a damper on any desire to be a homemaker. The living room had an old shag rug, filthy and full of God knows what remnants of the haunted horrors of that place.

To continue our once-romantic tradition, we slept in the living room between the speakers, placing Ben in the back room at night. He had no crib set up, and woke up in the night howling, crawling to the living room to sleep with us. Ben rarely ever cried, but he could feel that the house was haunted. He was a barometer for the abnormal.

Karen, our hippie friend from Marin, came to visit one day. She slept out on the porch for the fresh air. In the morning I suddenly rose in a waking dream, and I panicked. Tom was not in bed. An image flew into my mind of him out on the porch with Karen. I jumped out of bed, stumbled down the hallway and did not find him on the porch or in Ben's room. Everything went black, and in a cold sweat I sank down in the middle of the hall. Then nothing.

A flood of nausea swept over me as I sank back into my body and someone turned the sound back on. I was moaning, and I heard strange voices as ambulance men lifted me onto a stretcher. There were sirens as they sped the twisting roads to Santa Cruz. In the emergency room they hooked me to an IV. "Have you ever had heart trouble? What was going on right before this happened? We're testing your blood for diabetes."

"It's nothing. I just got up too fast. I was half asleep."

Tom stood by watching with a look on his face I couldn't read. Did he suspect the truth—that it was my crazy fear of losing him, the fear so great that I had some kind of catatonic fit? We drove home in silence. The world was soaked. The banks of Highway 9 were beginning to slide. Everything was coming apart.

Later Karen told me, "You just sat there bolt upright in the hallway staring straight ahead with glazed eyes, frozen as a corpse. You couldn't see or hear. It was scary. We thought you were having a stroke."

It rained and it rained, and I longed for Paradise Lost.

One day in a red sports car, Billy Mack, the bad boy, showed up. I had no idea how he knew where we were. (He was, after all, Hermes, the Trickster). He just wanted to check out our new digs, he said. He returned the next week with several weird people including a thin woman in a black velvet dress buttoned up the front. She talked me into giving her all my favorite clothes. She scared me, had a power. She must have been a witch.

Ben was teething. Billy Mack said that rubbing a little cocaine on his gums would help. I let him. Then he offered me a line. I said okay. In two hours time I threw together a whole darkroom, a bit wonky but workable.

The weird people stayed a few days. They were junkies. This house attracted junkies. Things began to disappear—first the television. Then, when we weren't at home, the enlarger disappeared from the darkroom. Emotional blackmail. Billy Mack knew he had a hold on me, that he could do whatever he wanted because of our little love secret.

Tom returned from work. He had had enough. He stood up straight, let his anger rip, and threatened to call the cops if they didn't leave. Billy Mack saw that he had no further business there. He left and we never saw him again.

At winter's end we found another place, a summer cabin, a tiny cracker box of a place. We had been lifted from the pit of hell into a little cube of sanity. The smallness didn't bother me a bit. It was fresh, cozy. There was light. It was spring. Yet, Tom and I passed each other in the tiny cabin and rarely talked. Nothing in this new world was friendly. Nothing safe.

And I could feel her. The Other Woman. She came to me in dreams. She was tracking. On her way. Sniffing around.

CHAPTER 3

House Model

TOM WAS A METALLURGICAL ENGINEER at Lockheed, analyzing metal failures on the Agena Missile. He had never studied architecture, nor had he ever drafted a house plan. In a few short months, he had done both.

This was no ordinary luxury house like one you might find in the suburbs; it was much more grandiose than the one my parents designed for a family of eight. Tom's house would have floors heated from below by a system of subfloor heated rocks; the Bozaks would be built into the walls of the rounded living room—a perfect theater of sound; a two-story chimney would serve as fireplace in the living room, provide fire for the kitchen's copper-hooded indoor BBQ, and upstairs, it would open to a fireplace in the master bedroom. And the *piece de resistance:* there would be a central vacuum system he had bought at an auction.

His plans were approved and stamped by a civil engineer who joked that the house was so overbuilt, the County probably wouldn't understand the details enough to take issue. There would be steel I-beams in the garage, fat redwood timbers that would be custom-milled by locals. The roof of copper sheeting would be a complexity of hills and valleys.

Everyone tried to talk Tom into a simpler house. The roof was impossible and expensive; the timbers were enormous. There would be more concrete poured into the foundation than in the Hoover Dam. "Make your first house a simple A-frame," advised a fatherly fellow worker at Lockheed who had built seven houses and knew what he was talking about. Tom listened politely.

As soon as the house plans were signed off, Tom began building a house model. Just as he had once sat carving, contour by contour, a 3-D replica of our hike through Glacier National Park, he now sat building a balsa wood house model intricately cut and engineered, tiny carved steps leading to the second floor bedrooms. With the model he could determine the exact angle of the afternoon sun through the large windows facing south. He calculated the size of the window frames so that the full vista of distant redwood mountains and sky would aesthetically fill the windows of the rounded house. The roof lifted off so you could see all the rooms from above.

The only way we could afford a house of this magnitude was to build it from used materials, and the best way to get them was to tear down houses. An ad in the San Jose Mercury offered a house for demolition for the price of one dollar. The contract: to remove the entire house and all debris in two months. Tom paid the dollar and they shook hands.

I found the demolition-woman challenge a welcome diversion, and also, therapeutic. I was strong; pounding on a building and tearing it apart was what I needed most in life. The house was a turn-of-the-century structure with two stories and a basement. There were lath and plaster walls, covered by three layers of wallpaper. Every weekend, armed with mallets, crowbars, hammers, cat's paws, and face masks, we tore at the house from sunup to sundown, stopping only to run to the Seven-Eleven for drinks and food. We parked Ben with a woman down the street.

I felt buoyant. I came to love the clean squeaking sound of molding as it was pried from the doorways. Lifting and tossing, banging and prying, I relaxed into the rhythm of the work. We pried up oak floorboards, saved the claw foot tub, the lath, the redwood boards, the bricks of the chimney. When nothing was left but the basement, we invited neighborhood people to sort through treasures, some from the early 1900's—clothes, bottles, books, and pictures.

And on the night we finished, once I had thrown down my crowbar; once we had arrived back home and dumped the pipes, wooden planks, lath, windows, bricks, sinks and tubs in the cabin's front yard; once I had laid Ben in his bed; once I had flopped onto our mattress, I whispered, "I like tearing down houses with you. It's the most fun we've had together since forever. I want to celebrate. Love me, Tom."

We kissed, stirring up wells of buried feeling. Tom ran his poor bruised hands over my breasts and down to the wetness between my legs, and we came together in a slow, quiet familiar swirl of passion. "It's all there, still there," I cried. "I really miss us. I miss the music and the loving and everything."

He kissed me and said teasingly, "You like this working together? You want more houses to tear down? I think I can arrange that."

White Raven,
When we hacked apart that house back then, I didn't think beyond the thrall of sheer destruction, the lust of salvage, the fun of working with Tom. Only now, years later, do I stop to think about the soul of that house. We peeled through four layers of wallpaper: roses, green-striped, yellow-flowered, every layer a step back into history. Only now do I see a phantom woman in long brown dress with cinched waist, chestnut hair piled up in a soft bun, as she leaves the parlor and lights a sconce in the hallway on her way to the flower-papered room upstairs where her child sleeps. And outside, streetcars rattle down St. James Street carrying men with handlebar mustaches and round straw hats. We peeled away that house's history, ripping nails that shrieked as they were jerked from the fiber of first-growth redwood where they had been locked for a hundred years.

CHAPTER 4

White Picket Fence

ONE DAY WHEN TOM WAS at work, a young woman came knocking on the door with a babe on her hip. She was petite, with a strong mouth, dark eyes and a black forest of hair—a mane of long thick wildness. She stood straight and poised as a dancer, and said in a girlish voice, "Hi. I'm Tamar. That old claw foot bathtub in your yard, is it for sale? I live in a house up on Fern Street across the way, and we could sure use a tub."

Carrying Ben on my back, I walked up Fern Street with her to a small white house that she and her husband Charles were renting. He was anticipating getting custody of his four children from his previous marriage. "Picture a white picket fence in front, said Tamar. "I already have the pickets. It will be cute."

Tamar was from Flushing, New York. She had come to California in the 60s, and met Charles in Big Sur at a Joan Baez concert. She was dancing wild and their eyes met. They were true hippies, living at Esalen, the institute famous the world over for spiritual practices, mind-body workshops, and the hot-spring mineral baths. They were married in Big Sur on a hill—she, six months pregnant in a white dress with an eyelet bodice from which her long dark pregnant nipples kept poking through, she told me with a giggle.

Later she brought Charles over to meet me. He was almost as short as Tamar, wore overalls, was bald on top with long hair hanging down in back. He stared straight into me with his cosmic blue Ram Das eyes and said with soft conviction, "We've known each other for a very, very long time."

When Tom met Tamar, only for a passing moment did the jealous question mark in my brain flash and glow. It was the easy way Tom and Tamar smoked pot together. The way she moved in her hippie skirts and tossed her long wild hair.

Tamar and I became best friends—the way sixth grade girls become best friends forever. We hung out in town, did our wash together at the village laundry, played with our one-year-old boys in the rec hall park, and she would leave her one-year-old, Ian Skye, with me for two hours a week while she played guitar and sang to children at the public school.

Tamar knocked on my door one day, and invited me to go to the county fair in Watsonville. "There's a costume contest with a children's theme and there's a prize for the best costume."

"I guess I'll wear my wedding dress. It's the only costume I have," I said.

"Cool. That's what I'm wearing too. I'm going to be "The White Thought," and I'll be pushing Skye in a buggy."

The day of the fair Tamar pulled up in "Frog," their old green Ford truck. Her black-bearded friend Garuda came too, dressed in a tie-dye shirt. We smoked a joint on the way. The moment we entered the gates of the fair I knew this was no place for stoned hippies. The county fair was still the bastion of American values pre-60s, and we giggled our way through the stalls of 4-H pigs and stands of apple pies and home-made jams.

When it came time for the costume contest, Garuda and I sat in the front row, and the parade began: multiple Mickey and Minnie Mice, Raggedy Anns, Goofys, and Howdy Dowdys, and finally, following the rear end of a horse came the White Thought—Tamar twirling a white parasol, pushing the white buggy with Ian Skye in a white diaper. Her long dark nipples that protruded from the eyelet bodice of her wedding dress pointed her way across the stage.

She did not win as she was sure she would, having the only really creative costume. She was mad all the way home. "I can't believe I didn't win, not even honorable mention! What's with these people?"

In Big Sur in her Esalen days, Tamar worked with Fritz Perls, the famous psychotherapist who coined the phrase "Gestalt Therapy." "Anastrophic expectations," Perls used to call this—the lack of coping with high expectations gone wrong. It was one of Tamar's notable charms.

That winter we had to move again. We rented the summer cabin of an old Italian couple. Mrs. Granucci was fat and stately, her gray hair neatly pinned up. Mr. Granucci was tall, thin, and quiet. They had never rented their cabin out before and were nervous, but Mrs. Granucci was won over by Ben's golden curls and Tom's good job. They agreed.

Soon, Tom was changing all the furniture around and in the process, a glassed picture was broken. Then all the building materials from the cabin on Big Basin were transported to the Granuccis' front and back yards. I cringed. I protested. I knew this would be trouble.

After that first house in San Jose, we had become demolition hounds. We tore down three more houses, inviting other pioneering friends in Boulder Creek to work with us and share the spoils. Tamar came once just to save the geraniums in the yard. We took apart a bathhouse in up-scale Atherton for three tons of slate flooring. There was a constant supply of new treasures: old toilets, unruly piles of naily lumber, barn wood, fence wire, windows, pipe, stone and bricks, tiles and roofing—all dumped into the Granuccis' yard.

I pulled my back lifting gigantic pieces of slate and loading them onto the truck. So much pain, and there was never time to heal—always more lifting. Always more pain, and the pain settled into my hips like a straightjacket.

In the fall the Granuccis pulled up in front of their house, unannounced. I watched from the living room window as they emerged from their car and looked around. Mrs. Granucci staggered and fell into a lawn chair. As I approached, she held her chest and croaked, "What is this? What have you done? This is our summer home. What have you done?"

I was sure she was having a heart attack. I brought her water. I tried to console her, apologizing over and over. I told her we would get rid of the piles. She was grief-stricken. Inside the house, she picked up the glassed picture that Tom had broken, and sighed. Twenty-five years of family memories shattered. The next day we received a notice of eviction to vacate the premises at once.

They came again a week later. Mrs. Granucci stood in front of the fireplace, her back to the fire, lifting her skirts and fanning the warmth with it. "I am a Christian woman," she began. "I am sorry for your having to move with the baby. You may have a month to get ready. But everything must be back in its place. This is a terrible thing for us. But I am a Christian."

We hired an excavator to cut the entryway onto our land. Crippled with back pain, I again lifted wood and bricks, slate, boards, and tubs, and it was all delivered at the base of our hill where, after the winter rains, the grasses grew tall and tangled in the spoils of our labor.

CHAPTER 5

Mountain People

In trailers they put mirrors everywhere
to trick the lack of space
and make it bigger

I am tall
I see the top of my head
scraping the ceiling
In the narrow mirror above the bed,
I see my elbows
washing dishes

WE CLEARED OUT OF THE Granuccis' yard, leaving it the same as we found it except for the smashed ferns lying face down on the ground. We bought a thirty-five-foot-long mobile home from an old couple who were breaking up, and had it hauled to Forest Glen Trailer Court a quarter mile down China Grade Road from our land. It was the only trailer court that allowed old cheap trailers and kids—in other words a ghetto of miscreants stuck together in close proximity, the only thing in common being the lack of money and the having of kids. Ben and the others would ride their tricycles up and down the trailer court between the sand piles at one end and the laundry room at the other.

There weren't more than four feet between the trailers. The man and woman next to us were fighting all the time and she would stand under our window wailing about his infidelities. There was no way not to listen. At Forest Glen Trailer Court there wasn't much we didn't know about each other.

Millie, in the coach across from us, became my trailer buddy. She was California Indian, and once a year she went to Oroville where her tribes would congregate for a powwow, drink acorn tea, hunt, tan deer hides, weave baskets and do bead work. She and her husband, also Native American, had a fierce but loving relationship. He was always threatening to leave because she couldn't keep the place clean. And she couldn't. Once when he was on the verge of leaving her, she called me, crying. She handed me a rake and in hysterics we raked the floor, hiding piles of stuff in garbage cans, saving her marriage once again.

Our trailer was a vintage old model with cherry wood cabinets, one bedroom in the back and a bathtub the size of a large drawer. As usual, we slept in the living room, and the bedroom in the back filled with things. Our hand-made pillows were the furniture.

After we met Tamar and Charles, other friends came easily. These mountains were attracting people from all parts of the country. People I could talk to. Ex-professionals, college-educated people: a techie morphing into an astrologer; a corporate physicist becoming a backwoods author of Double Day bestsellers on quantum physics.

One day a woman named Alexandra knocked on my trailer door, wondering if we wanted a kitten. (We didn't.) She and her husband Gary had just arrived from Baltimore and had bought land nearby. By her side stood Shawn, a curly blond about Ben's age. Their place was on a gentle hill up a road off our road, China Grade. It was a spreading piece of land with shady glens, a frog pond, oak trees sprinkled around, and meadows for orchards and gardens.

There was already a structure standing at the high point of their land, an abandoned shack once used by locals for blowing glass hash pipes. The shack was now the temporary home for Alexandra, Gary, and Alex's two kids from a previous marriage—the plan being to transform the shack into a house.

I was envious of their land—hidden away, private. Ours, a treeless hill, was so exposed, so extraverted for someone like me, a bred-in-the-bone introvert—one who is comfortable only in a corner table of a restaurant.

CHAPTER 6

Center Post I

As if planning an impossible house were not enough, we began planning our second child. Ben was planned around mountain trekking, and this baby would be our homesteading hippie child. It is good to tell your children that they were planned. What I didn't plan was that I would one day soon go crazy.

This child was conceived on the big green furry love cushion in the trailer. The plan was that she would also be born on this bed. But there was no way I was birthing my child in Forest Glen Trailer Court, and my mission in life was getting the trailer onto our land before the home birth.

Karen, our Marin friend, by this time, had found her calling as a midwife. She was attracted to the Birth Center, an underground organization of midwives holding prenatal appointments in an old Victorian in Santa Cruz. Once when I was there for a prenatal visit, a policeman came up the walkway and all the pregnant women hid in the bushes of the backyard.

Those were the days of hippie births in tepees and shacks. Tribal births with drumming and incense, music and celebration. Karen was working in San Francisco, awaiting my call that our baby was on the way. This would be her first witnessed birth. She would be there.

When I was seven months pregnant Tom, Ben and I drove up to Downieville in Gold Country where Tom had read about a lumber mill being torn down. Tom was searching for the perfect twelve-by-twelve, twenty-two-foot long post for the apex of the living room, out of which would radiate a spoke-wheel of beams. We arrived in late morning, and were greeted by Elmer, a lanky man in his seventies, and his wife Maureen who was a comfortable, apple-pie sort of wife. They had a cheery, sunny old house. They invited us for lunch.

Elmer had been a hard-working man. You could see it in the thick veins standing out on his forearms and in his lean muscular frame. You could tell that his whole life had been the sawmill. He just got too old, and now his project was to tear it all down, piece by piece, and sell the timbers. He and Tom connected. I believe he saw in Tom his younger self, a man full of drive, one who had come all the way to the north country to find the center post for our house.

After lunch we went over to the mill, what was left of it. Old-growth redwood timbers sat outside the building in neat stacks according to size. Tom spotted the timber he wanted. It was huge: more than twenty feet long; only problem—it was still a beam supporting the roof. Elmer promised to save it for us. Tom put money down and said he would be back in a couple of months when it was released from its job of holding up the old mill.

Elmer and his wife took quite a liking to us and were tickled that their timber would be immortalized as the center of our family's home.

At Lockheed there was a man named Craney who had a home in Riverside Grove near where the Granucci house sat. Craney's house was perched up a steep narrow road, and they called it "The Red Roost." On the lower land they had a horse corral and a large barn. Craney and his wife decided to leave Boulder Creek. "It's getting too crowded here," they said. "We're going to Wyoming—real cowboy country."

They sold the barn and surrounding land to a commune from Maine, a group of seven: two couples, a sister and brother, and a single woman named Barbara. Fresh from the snows of Maine, they found themselves knee-deep in Boulder Creek mud.

Barbara would stand on the deck in the early morning in her woolen cap, wearing the same clothes she had had on yesterday. "It's too cold to change clothes. What's the point?" She would position herself, pelvis jutting forward, and pee a straight stream right off her deck like any man.

The people from Maine moved into Craney's big barn, put up shelves, put in a wood stove, kitchen sink, built outhouses, and they all lived communally in the barn. Eventually, they spread out on the land into small cabins, and the barn became the central gathering place. We called them the Barn People.

The exact time of our move to the land had not been planned. One day the Barn People came by and Barbara said, "Why not now? What's wrong with today?" Tom looked at me and I looked at him and it was settled. We had no trailer hitch. At the trailer park our one-ton white Chevy truck was married to the trailer with chains and ropes going this way and that under and over and through. Tom who never did anything without research and development was like a kid on a dare. He knew that he would need plenty of momentum to get the trailer over the lip at the base of the driveway. He cut away the fence bordering the wide, open field across the road.

Back at Forest Glen Trailer Court, he climbed into the driver's seat and the rig began its slow crawl down China Grade Road. He turned right into the field, swung a wide circle so that the front of the truck was heading straight for our driveway, revved the engine and tore across the field, whipping across the road and banging over the lip of the driveway and onto the land.

The trailer landed like a beached whale in the field down below. The excavator had cut and graveled the driveway at a 30% grade, switchback and all, to the top of the hill where the house would stand one day. The trailer should have been dragged up the hill, but it seemed, for reasons I didn't understand, that "all the king's horses and all the king's men" could not get it up there now.

I fully expected it to arrive there in time for the birth, but in those days, expectation and life were taking different routes. And so our home became the flat open field of the lower land, just behind the poison oak brush that bordered China Grade, just beside the dumping ground where all the spoils of demolition were delivered. That is where we landed, and that is where we stayed.

The percolation and septic permits had been approved, and the father of all septic tanks, one large enough for three bathrooms, was driven up the newly carved driveway and lowered into the ground. Mazel Tov! At least something had managed to get to the top.

The whale-size septic tank was neatly buried up on the hill, empty and useless, but down at the bottom was nothing but an open field. No running water, no outhouse, no heat, and no privacy. Tom dug a hole under the trailer where the toilet would drain.

Something happened to me when he dug that hole. Here was a trailer sitting like a rock, immobilized in a hot empty field. I realized at that moment that nothing I thought, desired, or did would make a bit of difference. We were falling into a black hole called "temporary," and I began to lose any confidence that he, my husband and father of our children, would champion our needs. He dug a hole for us. I began the descent, began to give up. And that was not a good state of mind for a woman about to give birth.

Our pioneering effort was not the communal sort, as with the Barn People from Maine or up on Harmony Hill where folks lived in cabins and yurts down private dirt roads, far from the critical eye of civilization. We sat there exposed, one mile past the Boulder Creek Golf and Country Club and in plain view of the house down the road—once Old Mrs. Crawford's, now owned now by her daughter and son-in-law.

It was August. We lived there in the field vulnerable, nothing to hide us, in dirt and sweat—and then came the heat of late summer. The days grew hot and hotter. You stick a metal box out in the middle of a dry and windless field with no trees anywhere, turn the temperature up one degree at a time until it is one hundred, inject ten thousand flies into it, and you have a perfect torture chamber.

CHAPTER 7

Ten Thousand Flies

I WAS SITTING IN A lounge chair by the trailer in the shade of the shed full of scrounged wood and wire, waiting for the baby to arrive. Tom had a handle on it this time and was not sitting by my side on the due date, watching for the labor lights to go on. He was busy.

For two days I went into hard labor that petered out by nightfall. Karen came from San Francisco. This birth would be her entrance exam to the Birth Center of Santa Cruz.

Alexandra who lived down the road guessed that the baby wasn't coming because the nights were cool and we had no source of heat. She found an old Ben Franklin wood burner at the thrift shop and our Born Again Christian neighbor, Jack, set it up. This birth was becoming a neighborhood event. The next day my labor settled in and stuck.

Karen sat with me in the field in the unforgiving (I will never forgive it!) heat of mid October. In the afternoon we escaped to Big Basin Redwood Park five miles up China Grade, and sat on the banks of Huckleberry Creek in the natural air conditioning of redwoods that draw in tons of water from the earth, exuding a fine mist into the air. I labored in the park until I could walk no more.

The midwives came in the cool of evening. Tamar arrived bearing bread and wine. She held Ben on her lap. Tom kept busy flapping sheets around and finally settled in beside me on the bed. The fire was crackling and the birthing sheets were spread. Alexandra and Gary arrived just before the birth. The flies, still active in the warm evening, were watching and waiting.

Transition came fast and I felt her coming.

"Slowly. Slow it down," they said, so you won't tear."
"How? How? The baby wants to come!"
Breathe with me," said Karen.

Samantha Corn was delivered to us in the quiet of evening, in the light of oil lamps and candles glowing, with the smell of incense in the air and roses in the vase above the bed. Trailer Baby Sam. And I kept her on my breast her first world night and repeated like a chant, "I'll always be your mommy. I'll always be your mommy."

With midwives, with water boiling on the wood burning stove, with wine, incense, candles and a circle of friends. . . there was no question anymore. We were true hippies.

Sami was passed around the room and we drank wine and broke bread. The midwives placed the placenta in a bowl, and the apple tree given to us by the Barn People from Maine was to be planted over it tomorrow. Tomorrow.

And when tomorrow came. . . I woke up to find a dehydrated baby on my chest. Ben was sitting there watching her, saying "That's got a small hand." Tom woke up and went to work. Karen needed to return to her job up in the city. The flies woke up and began their morning buzz against the windows, discussing their plans for the day.

I laid the baby down, grabbed a broom and swept out the trailer. I gathered the bloody sheets and bundled them into the back room. I went into the bathroom, peed in the toilet and heard it landing in the hole below the trailer. Ben pooped in the potty and the flies rushed there. On the sink I saw a bowl of black liver covered with fly eggs. "What's that??" I shrieked, and remembered the sacred placenta. I wrapped it in newspaper and threw it in the garbage. The party was over.

Alexandra came by later and rescued me—again. I was still sticky with the birthing blood, and we drove up to Big Basin Park which had public showers. She held my baby as I stood in the shower, hot water cascading over me, while Ben and Alex's son Shawn played in the trees.

We went to town and I sat on the bench in front of Erba's Market, people stopping by to see a one-day-old baby, wondering what I was doing out and about.

Mom and Dad were relieved now that the home birth was over and I was still in one piece (two to be exact). They flew to San Francisco to see their new granddaughter, rented a car, pulled into the driveway and took it all in. I'm sure they had hoped for a decent pastoral scene. After all, Tom and I were both college-educated middle-class kids. My mother couldn't speak. She stood in the trailer fanning flies from Sami's face and finally, breaking her policy of non-interference, she blurted out, "You could come home and stay with us, just for awhile—just until things improve here. Come home, Laurie."

"It'll be better soon. You'll see. We'll be okay."

They stayed only one hour. As they were leaving, I stood in the field in my long blue dress holding my screaming baby, trying so hard to be an outstanding hippie. My mother who was trying so hard not to interfere, said, in a voice both loving and firm, "Laurie, take care of yourself."

"I'm all right," I said.

It was then she spoke the words I have heard over and over all these years: "Laurie, there's more to life than being all right." And they stepped into their car and were gone.

My mom used to say, when a piece of meat was too gristly, too tough to chew, "Just suck the goodness out of it." I have always done that. I have sucked the goodness out of the sinewy past, rolled it around, digested it, and the gristle turned to honey.

Years after the death of my mother, my father told me that on that day they left me standing in the field, Mom cried all the way to the airport, as well she should have. I romanticized those days. . . made honey of the past. But in that pot of honey is a swarm of flies so raucous and profuse I can still hear them buzzing—zinging like tiny trapped bullets around the chambers of my brain.

Shocking! shrieks The White Raven. The day after a home birth in a trailer, the father gets up and leaves for work while I was left with bloody sheets, no plumbing, no hot water to bathe, a three-year old, a newborn, and flies everywhere. And my parents were coming to visit?

Is there any more grotesque image than a placenta, the blessed afterbirth, covered in white eggs—the life-giving placenta giving life to the flies, the ten thousand tormentors of my life?

Who was this man who left for work? Who was this woman that she could pick herself up and grab a broom and sweep the floor? She was married to the 70s—tried to excuse this as normal hippie behavior, and paraded it before her parents who knew that she knew better.

What made this man and woman wander so far from the broad range of normalcy? He was a metallurgist at Lockheed analyzing material fractures with a scan electron microscope. In the City they had lived in an opera of love and passion. Tom was not a mean person; he was a clueless, charming eccentric with a big dream.

But it was a male dream. He was building for eternity—a monument to himself. And the woman? The introvert who didn't like to stand out—sitting exposed in a field where she felt the whole world pointing fingers?

This man and this woman were becoming lost to one another—he in his lonely quest to build a house, she in her inability to grasp that as an adult, as a mother, she was becoming a model of dysfunction.

CHAPTER 8

Trailer Baby Sam

Inter urinas et faeces nascimur -
Between pee and shit we are born

I DON'T KNOW EXACTLY WHEN I started to go crazy. It was gradual, like a slow death, and no one really knew. It was not a flipping-out kind of crazy—but a narrowing, a tightening of the world around me when the air grew thick and heavy and hazy and breathing did not come easily.

I would have flashbacks to a far-away world, back to the Land of Childhood, lying in an open field smelling the crackling grasses of a Midwest summer and watching huge fluffy clouds drift across the lazy blue. I would have flashbacks of shopping centers or a walk through tree-arched streets to the university, and it seemed like a lost empire, a sublime and enchanted world.

When you contain a mob of flies inside a jar and open the jar, only a few smart ones leave. The others think they are stuck in there. I was as dumb as the flies, buzzing from one end of my metal cage to the other. And all I had to do was walk out the door. Except that there was no car. Our VW bug was up on blocks waiting for repairs. Like a caged animal, I paced back and forth in the suffocating heat, flies busy in the air, holding a screaming babe to my tit while Ben sat in the corner chanting, "Make her stop, Mommy. Make her stop."

Baby Sam wrung her tiny hands and her ancient face knew everything. She cried every moment she wasn't held. Someone had given me a baby swing and I discovered that the swinging put her to sleep. I can still hear that cranked up swing ticking—back and forth, back and forth.

I didn't understand that I could just take a break, rent a small cabin nearby, go home to Toledo for a while. The trailer walls were the boundaries of my life, and I pounded on them every day screaming, "Get me out of here! Get me out of here!"

If you were in our trailer facing China Grade Road, you would see, adjacent to our field on the left, a sweet, cheery little house with blue shutters and a grassy lawn with a fuzzy black dog running around. Jack and Jessica lived there with their three children, and another on the way. They had just found Jesus and were "be fruitful and multiply" Good News Christians who took an interest in the strange goings-on in the field next to their land. Jack was the one who had helped Alexandra install the wood-burning Franklin stove the day before Sami's birth.

They must have heard me pounding and screaming from time to time. I'm sure everyone on that road must have heard me, but as self-conscious as I was, I must have been too crazy to care. Sometimes I wonder if I was really screaming, or just thought I was. It hardly matters. There is no doubt that in that dog-days summer heat I had gone quite mad.

I should not tell you everything. Some things are better left unsaid. Too embarrassing. Too personal.

I should not tell you: that because there was no outhouse—building one would have been acknowledging the permanence of our "temporary" situation—we wrapped our shit in newspaper and put it in the garbage; that the wrapping went from days to weeks to months; that when Tom went to work, sometimes he left his shit wrapped in newspaper on top of the useless relic of a toilet. Mine was in the trashcan. Ben's was in the potty. Sami's was in her diapers. Pee and shit. Shit and pee. And the flies were everywhere.

I should not tell you. . .that our Good News neighbor Jack crossed the field one day to say that his dogs were pulling the shitty newspapers out of our trash, nosing around in them, and then returning home to lick their master's face.

Pee and shit, shit and pee. That was my day. But I should not tell you. Some things are better left unsaid.

One day Jack and Jessica came over and invited us to stay for a week in their home while they went out of town. We had only to feed their dog. It was a tiny, simple, unpretentious house. The second I set foot in it, it was as if my dazed eyes slowly swam into focus on a world that looked exactly as it should have looked. There was a sunny kitchen with a gas stove, spice shelves, a wooden table with matching chairs all around. There were white curtains on the bedroom windows. There was a washer-dryer, for God's sake.

I laid Sami on the bed and changed her diaper, no mob of flies to accost us, and she didn't cry. Ben was in the living room pushing his cars and trucks around, and Tom was on the front porch reading a "Scientific American." From the living room window I could look across to our trailer, a gleaming cauldron in the afternoon sun. I turned away.

All that week I felt like my mother, doing simple mother things: laundry, cooking dinner, putting it on the table, singing to my baby at night. All that week I was in an ecstasy of tears, and in terror of the day they would return.

And when that day arrived and we moved back into the hellhole in the field next door, I sank back into a dazed and quiet despair. I came undone, wishing almost that we had never had that week.

My milk was drying up. With Ben I had been a milk factory, my shirts always wet with the overflow. It wasn't that I had no milk, but I couldn't let it down and the supply diminished. Sami screamed and screamed and her skin broke out in eczema. I carried her to a neighbor who lived on the other side of Jack and Jessica. She had recently birthed her second child, and I sat holding her son as she nursed Baby Sam. I sat there in my daze picturing my mother lining up sterilized bottles on the kitchen counter, pouring warm formula into them and capping them with the sterilized nipples.

For two weeks I had to run to my wet-nurse neighbor, but soon my milk returned— an adequate stream, just enough. Barely enough.

CHAPTER 9

Dream House

OUR FINANCES WERE IN PLACE to build the house—that is to say my father lent us the money. It was the Barn Men from Maine who were hired. They offered to work for $5.00 an hour, a dollar less than the wage for building tract homes in San Jose. They preferred the challenge of a real mountain home, and it would be solid work for months to come.

The ground was staked and ready. Only the final building permit was required. Tom begged permission from the higher-ups at Lockheed Missiles and Space to work two days a week while the house was under construction. The Cold War would have to go on without him.

He began smoking pot all day. You can't blame him. He had the endless task of de-nailing all the two-by-fours from the demolished houses. Piece by piece. suspended between two sawhorses, with cat's paw and crowbar, he freed the nails. He smoked and pried. Pried and smoked. That was his day.

The morning the building permit arrived, the Beautiful Men from Maine showed up, posted the permit, put up a temporary power pole, broke champagne, and Ben, standing there with the men, announced:

"They're building the house model now."

Concrete was poured and the outline of the rounded house was formed. A stairway was constructed from the garage level up to the first floor. The chimney that would serve both the first and second floor fireplaces was completed.

Tom was father to a slowly growing house. It was his. I was mother to two fast-growing children. They were mine. Tom's vision propelled the Beautiful Men from Maine who worked bare-chested in the sun. From down in the trailer I could hear the pounding of nails echoing through the mountains, the shouts, the laughter of men at work.

And down below I was pounding the trailer walls. My life was a maddening monotone, propelled by the details of survival—shopping, garbage, diapers, nursing, shit and pee, and somehow putting a meal together.

The first time Ben heard me scream he stood frozen, and from that moment on he was lost in the haze, not knowing how to act. In the innocence of a curious three-year-old he hovered over me diapering Sami, trying to help, getting in the way. I screamed at him. I slapped his hands.

And there was the time when Mandy across the street invited us to a Thanksgiving party. I offered to make pumpkin pies. I was hyper in the kitchen trying to do just one normal thing. I was pouring the filling into the pie plates with Ben beside me, balanced on the green wicker stand. The pie plates were upset, the mixture dribbling down the stove to the floor. I shrieked. Ben went running to the other end of the trailer and I threw the green wicker stand. I didn't mean for it to hit him, but it did. He stood there cowering like a puppy and in a hushed voice announced, "You threw that chair at me."

I fell apart. I held him to me sobbing, hoping that this would not be one of those childhood memories locked away. Poor Ben with his sweet, black face—his nose never stopped running—and mixed with the dirt of the field where he played, his face was permanently coated with black snot. He looked like a young miner home from the mines. I tried to keep it clean. Believe me I tried, but it was no use. I would have been wiping every five minutes, rubbing him raw.

I stayed. I didn't go anywhere. I was zombie numb, stumbling through the day. If I had been hit by a logging truck on China Grade it wouldn't have mattered. If it hadn't been for my children I wouldn't have cared.

> *Oh! My children!*
> *You keep me stuck to this life*
> *finding your shoes*
> *cleaning your clothes, wiping your faces*
> *wiping your hands*
> *Without you I might splinter and fall into a pile of shards*
> *and wash away in the next rain.*
> *Love, Mom*

If there was once a Zone Called Paradise, this was the Zone Called Hell. Unhealthy, humiliating, stinking, buzzing world that in my stunned mind I dared to believe was temporary. No wonder I went into a mental haze, a state of torpor. Why did I act as if I were being chained to the trailer with ankle fetters, with two deprived children who were always getting lice, scabies, pinworms? Why did he not pull the trailer up the driveway and connect it to the septic tank that sat up there, virginal and waiting. Why did I leave it all to him?

I cared about the house in an abstract way. It was some kind of condition of life. As long as the Beautiful Men from Maine were up there pounding nails, the house was a vision and a promise. He was moving toward the vision with blinders on. For him, there was no weight, no real validity to the flytrap of a trailer that was a temporary thing.

But me? I lived in the temporary. And I was flaking, breaking—trapped in a metal box with a baby on my tit and a depressed three-year-old blithering in the corner. I raged and paced back and forth, as in a Greek tragedy—a writhing chorus of the furies screaming "Get me out of here!"

But I stayed.

White Raven,

It has struck me more than once that there was a moment in time that was the beginning of all this submissiveness—that moment in the chair of the plastic surgeon in Chicago when I let a perfect stranger, a monster-of-a-man, tell me how he would alter my face. Was I really in the grip of an enchantment?

I want an easy answer to why I became a woman who could fall into such weakness, degradation and belittlement. I want to believe that after that trauma, I kept reliving the act of going under the knife, but in different ways—with a rapist, with this self-absorbed, scary, driven man—my submissiveness possessing me like a dark spell, straight from the unconscious. I want to believe there's a fairy tale answer to why I was so broken.

dream house
mountain fortress of redwood timbers
a house crazy with size

I am fragile as a bird
My chest is shell-thin against the universe
    God, why did you give me bubbles
    instead of breath

Tom, I am not dancing. I am not

CHAPTER 10

Comes The Buddha

JENNA AND RUSSELL RIVERS CAME with their baby from British Columbia where they had lived an idyllic life on a small island near Vancouver. They had found their teacher, Tbuten Yeshe, an exalted Tibetan lama, and they were looking to start a spiritual community. They came to Boulder Creek to find their old friends, Tamar and Charles, and together the two families bought a piece of land in the backwoods of Boulder Creek—eighty acres of virgin forest at a good price.

With Sami on my hip I hiked to the top with Charles and Tamar. The way was steep, especially near the top where we climbed rocks and clung to trees. At the top: a stunning view of the Santa Cruz Mountains. A hawk was circling above. This was not where Tamar pictured her cute little house with a white picket fence. This was a one-third-mile hike straight up a steep mountain. There was no way to get there but to walk. No way to bring things up but to carry them. The winters would be hard. They named the upper acres Omland.

A path was laid. Jenna carved steps into the earth, from the bottom to the top. Benches were placed along the way. By the bottom creek, a large red ladle hung for visitors to drink. Up the mountains were carried all of life's provisions: chairs, beds, chain saws, wood burning stoves, garden tools, hoses, books, kerosene lamps.

Russell and Jenna lived in a pyramid structure. Tamar and Charles put up a tepee, planted flowers all around, and the white pickets finally found their home. An outhouse, "the shitter," with five rickety steps was built, with a bucket of sawdust next to the carved and sanded seats. A terraced garden with Hollyhocks and vegetables grew with the help of Charles's meticulous arrangement of hoses. At the top of the garden sat "Gertie," the old wringer-washer.

The communal meeting place, the kitchen, was a yurt-like structure, open on the sides with canvas roll-down walls, a shake roof, a dirt floor, cupboards, the cooler (a hole in the ground with wooden cover), and a water line connecting the sink and outside shower to the spring reservoir farther up the mountain. Toys and books and drums were stashed on shelves around the kitchen, and kerosene lamps hung from the poles. Little altars were set into niches, with feathers, candles and pictures of Swami Muktananda, Tamar's and Charles's guru from their ashram days. It was here outside the kitchen that Tamar transplanted the geraniums she had rescued from a house we tore down in San Jose. In the center of the kitchen was a huge redwood table with graffiti carved by teenagers and guests.

Charles who had received custody of the four children from his previous marriage had transported them from the suburbs of San Mateo to this mountaintop. Amongst them there were varying degrees of acceptance, but they all agreed on one thing: the steep part of the hike near the top was to be named "the fucker." The teenagers lived down a slope beyond the kitchen and called their neck of the Omland woods "the mental ward."

Bells and chimes hung from trees and bird feeders sat outside the walls of the kitchen. Jasmine vines climbed the trellis near the outside table where food was spread at Omland parties, held on summer and winter solstice.

As the months passed Jenna and Russell began to envision something more. Seeking a greater community, they met with other followers of Lama Yeshe, and decided to give the lower portion of the land to a new settlement for California Tibetan Buddhists. Jenna and Russell, now pregnant with their second, moved down the mountain, and Russell built a small structure on the rise above base camp, just in time for the birth.

Karen, now the midwife of the backwoods, arrived. It was a hot day and as Jenna calmly labored—slowly, quietly, people began to congregate at the edge of the birth scene until there were twenty people looking on. Jenna birthed her second daughter, quietly, on hands and knees. It was only afterwards that she and Russell looked around, surprised to see that they had performed a tribal birth.

The Buddha had come to the backwoods. The lower land became the Vajrapani Institute, drawing followers of Lama Yeshe from San Diego, Berkeley, and Los Angeles. A *gumpa* (temple) was built by volunteers and painted in the colors of Tibetan Buddhism. Prayer flags were strung outside the temple and structures began to form on the land and up Deer Creek. The road leading to Vajrapani was graded and graveled. The backwoods of Boulder Creek became a retreat and teaching center for people from around the world. One day fifteen years later, the Dalai Lama himself would come to visit this land where Lama Yeshe's ashes now lay.

Omland, the upper acres, now Tamar's and Charles's, was home to their children, various homeless teenagers and other wandering hippie folk. When Tamar moved onto the land it was a totemic move. She who was barefoot in the Bronx now walked barefoot up her mountain. She called herself Sequoia Deer. Her hair was long and braided. She walked light-footed, straight and proud, up the mountain, and as she neared the top she would call an owl call to her husband and he would answer back. Her hands grew rough with ingrained dirt. Her feet grew tough as leather. She loved the quiet of the land and asked to be buried there someday.

Summer Solstice
Party at Omland Mountain

A trail of women with hip-slung babes, small children, Vajrapani people, and old folks trek up the mountain bearing fruit, corn, bagels, desserts and wine. When they reach the kitchen at the top they are offered water and a chair at the lookout place on the edge of the world. Great pots of corn are bubbling. Spaghetti sauce simmers on the wood burner. A kettle of chai is brewing. Smell of cardamom and star anise drift from the kitchen.

At the lookout place where distant mountains rise from the valleys below, people are singing and drumming. African thumb pianos, shakers, flutes, guitars and mandolin. Marijuana smoke mingles with the smell of chai and spaghetti.

Women are dancing. One takes off her top. People drift to the tepee into a circle of drums. Even those who have never drummed cannot escape the primordial trance.

Here on this Native American mountain
in this green and open place
where euphoria sweeps through
as natural as the warm breath of summer
people are dancing and drumming
unaware that someday this will be
a part of history

I was always on the periphery of Buddhism. The Buddha softened the edges of my human miseries, put them in perspective; they were merely the struggles of the self that lead to enlightenment, *n'est-ce pas?*

It seemed long ago—the days of that first house in Riverside Grove where we were robbed by heroin addicts and haunted by the ghosts of murdered drug dealers. We were moving from isolation to a more extroverted life. Everyone down all those dirt roads in "them thar hills" was doing it. We were counterculture people, brazen in our attempts to build without codes, to live in hovels, tepees, backwoods shacks.

True, we felt a part of something bigger than ourselves. But know this. Even in this "anything goes" hippie world, our trailer stood out on the far end of the normal spectrum.

We lived in two worlds—the larger one framed as the 70s, with the music, the magic, the spiritual communes, the feel-good parties. But there was a smaller world inside that bigger one: the hellhole, the fly trap of a trailer dripping pee into a cesspool—the scene that might not have made it into all those groovy books about the hippie era—books about hot-tubbing, free love, dancing, and naked love children.

Were there deeper forces that drove this man? Had he been a medieval king who was now compelled to build this massive rounded fortress high on a hill looking down on all the peasant dwellings below? And how would one build such a castle?? By pillaging and plundering the countryside below, tearing down houses, ransacking greenhouses, buying up old bridge timbers. That's how. Pillaging and plundering. Doing it again.

> *That is a fanciful (although perhaps valid) California explanation, says The White Raven. In mere psychological terms, Tom was inflated. He had an "edifice complex." How in the world did he, a twenty-eight-year-old who had never built a shelf, have the audacity to plan this mammoth house—and then refuse to take suggestions or advice from anyone (meaning almost everyone) who knew better? Why this hubris?*
>
> *The first time we stood at the top of the hill and took in the vista of redwood mountains cloaked in mist, Tom was transfixed. Was it the hill itself that seduced him? Did he hear sirens on that green hill, hypnotically singing? We may never know. The reasons are buried deep in the psyche and in the dust and debris of the half-built house.*

CHAPTER 11

Poverty

Transcendental Meditation

I was initiated into TM.
wore my long blue dress, brought my flower
paid my hundred dollars,
received my secret mantra

Twice each day
I would leave the children with Tom
sit in the metal shed
amidst the brick and wire and wood
to meditate.

I don't remember what happened in the shed
It doesn't matter
I had twenty minutes to myself
a miracle
that probably saved my life

THE FIRST SUMMER WAS OVER, and progress was good if you had two hundred years to build a house. Tom quit Lockheed altogether to work on it full-time. At his company farewell party he was given a leather holster and a hammer.

And so it was that the house "lumbered" along. The house had gone "Boulder Creek" where people didn't wear watches, and you were "country cool" if you were laid back and you were "city" if you were uptight and in a hurry. There were massive problems of lifting and hauling. Every hoisting of a redwood beam had to be engineered. Money was running out, and time didn't care.

There were I-beams in the garage holding up the first floor, so massive was the hulk of this great ship, afloat among the redwoods. The salvaged oak flooring had been laid, pounded into place by the Beautiful Men from Maine, taking the shape of the future rounded living room and the adjacent kitchen/dining room.

A party was announced to test the solidity of the floor, transplanted from the turn-of-the-century house in San Jose to an open-deck stage in the Santa Cruz Mountains. People came. They came in lines, like ants, from all over the hills. Alexandra and Gary, the Barn people from Maine, the Vajrapani folks, Tamar and Charles. They streamed up the driveway with bowls of food, with babies and drums. The giant Bozaks sat on the edge of the living room with no walls, and the music ripped into the country night.

We danced and drummed to Santana, to "Woodstock," The Rolling Stones, to "The Low Spark of High Heeled Boys." There were no walls but the circle of mountains. There was no ceiling but the night. The music bounced around the redwood mountains. Spinning, stomping, we danced, wave after wave, in one big mountain hippie high. Women whirling with long dresses and flying scarves—crazy with dance against the moon-full sky. I danced. They danced. We danced. You just had to be there.

I was there and I well remember. It was a magical scene, recalls the White Raven—but wait a minute. Wait a minute! He laid the oak floor before the walls and ceilings were secured? Absurd! Why didn't I notice back then? Didn't anyone know better? Did he think the structure would be completed before winter came? How frantic he must have been when the

> *rains came and he had to cover the vintage wood floor with plastic, and more plastic for all the winters to come. He was a smart man. What was he thinking?*

We were legally poor now. After Tom quit Lockheed we went on welfare and food stamps. Yet thousands of dollars had disappeared into the house, into materials bought from dealers or at auctions. Tom bought a commercial greenhouse, tore it down for the corrugated siding and the huge commercial fans. He bought weathered bridge timbers from a dealer in San Jose, railroad ties to terrace the hill for a future garden. He bought a restaurant-size double-oven gas stove. He went on buying.

Because I grew up with money I had never really felt poor or desperate, even if there was only a nickel in my pocket. The suburban shopping center was always just around the corner of my mind. But now: food stamps? MediCal? welfare? You who read this may resent that I was a welfare mama. I don't blame you. I resent me too. There were many of us sitting in the food stamp office on Emeline Street who shouldn't have been. It was like a party, with guitars and singing and little boys with runny noses hiding under chairs and little girls skipping around barefoot in flowered hippie dresses.

It was the times. It was easy. Where it wasn't easy was standing in the grocery line pulling out my food stamps, stealing sheepish glances at the straight housewife next in line. Every time I pulled them out I felt that I was insulting my parents, my aunts, uncles, cousins, the whole Jewish middle-class society of Toledo, not to mention the working people in California who paid taxes to support us and our poverty habit. But after all, how else were we to build this half-million dollar house, I ask you?

CHAPTER 12

Center Post II

There was a time
not long enough ago
when you would not be seen with me in town
when you would make excuses and walk away
You would sit on the bench
in front of Erba's market
pretending, wishing that I didn't exist
watching the women walk by
in their tight jeans, vulva outlined
tank tops swaying with
weighted breasts
wishing, pretending that you were free

As Tom worked on the house with the Beautiful Men from Maine, his body grew tight and muscular. He had lost his "city." He had a mountain man swagger and his beard and curls turned blond in the sun. He and the crew would go to town on lunch break, sit on the bench in front of Erba's Market and watch the flesh walk by. The Other Woman was a seductress on parade: tank-topped babes in barely-there crocheted halters and cut-off jeans shorts. Boulder Creek was a walking "Penthouse" gallery. On his lunch break, my husband went bachelor.

I looked as good in a tank top and short shorts as the rest of them. But for him, I had become a Monster of Need—a constant reminder of the house that grew more slowly than our children would ever grow. In town, he could, for just one hour of every day, be one of the guys drinking a beer on the bench in front of Erba's.

One day I was standing dazedly in the construction zone with Baby Sam in my arms, watching the Beautiful Men from Maine hoist the gigantic twenty-two-foot long center post into place with cables and winches. Suddenly the post came crashing down inches from where I stood. The men came rushing over. "Are you all right? That was so close. Did you see it coming?"

I didn't, and the strange thing is that I didn't feel anything, no adrenaline, no anything. My feelings were all used up. It was only later that night in bed that my heart started madly pounding and I saw that we were almost smashed, Baby Sam and I, immortalized there—our blood smeared forever on the center post of our house.

When Sami was a year old, we took a trip to Tassajara, a Zen retreat center in the Carmel Valley. It seems that when people are at the bottom of their marriages they go on vacation. They take trips to Zen Paradise. We rented a cabin, rose to the deep gong calling people to sit in meditation, ate famous Tassajara breads and organic feasts, and walked the trails to the rapids where naked bodies were draped across rocks in the rushing stream. People waded in the bubbling waters, laughing and talking softly in a Garden of Eden sort of way.

I sat on the rocks holding Sami while Tom did the wading. I was waiting for him to be nice, to take *our* baby off my hands so I could be free to walk around, to lie draped on a rock in the rapids, but he wasn't nice, and I was morose.

He was curiously energetic that night in the cabin. I wondered why, but didn't ask. The next day we left. We didn't talk all the way home.

CHAPTER 13

The Circle of Women

LIKE A LIONESS, I PACED back and forth in my cage—any creative impulse buried so deep that nothing could dredge it up, until one day Alexandra crossed the field, walked up the two steps into the trailer where I sat dazed on a pillow nursing Sami. She broke into my fog and said, "I worry about you. I think you should join a writing group with Ellen Bass. You'd love it, and the women are great."

I looked up surprised and said in a lifeless, droning voice, "I'm Okay. Everything will be okay. This will be over soon. We'll be up top. Have hot water. It'll be better."

"But how can you stand this? Tom does nothing for you. You're abandoned down here without even a car to drive."

"Tom's trying. He has lots on his mind and doesn't have the time to work on stuff down here."

"Stuff down here is all you have. He's busy and preoccupied, but you should expect the basics, just the basics. Water. Shelter. A toilet, for God's sake. You don't seem to care anymore."

I blinked and went on nursing. I didn't want to think too much. It was painful to think. Yes, and if I had had love I could have lived in a shack and eaten dirt. If I were cherished I could have been Earth Woman, hippie of the year. If there had been love. Without it I was a poor woman with a shrunken soul and a light that was flickering day by day in a fog that had settled dense and heavy in the eight-foot-wide cage of my world.

Writing group? It seemed absurd and impossible, stepping out of the confines of my numb and narrow world—finding my way to a sunny white house in Ben Lomond where a circle of women sat on the floor, where I was welcomed by a radiant young woman sitting lotus, with dark pony-tail and shining black eyes. I arrived with a throbbing headache and a pad of paper.

My heart jumped like Indian drums when I spotted in the circle an old friend whom I had forgotten. The Muse had gotten there before me, saved me a place, her long black hair (and a few silver ones) glistening, her eyes aglow, her pencil poised and ready to fly. I sat down next to her with my pad of paper, trembling hands—and once again. . .my life was saved.

It was the days of women's writing workshops, a time of the stirring of female consciousness. Ellen Bass was our guide. Her soft laughter would tell you if your writing hit it funny. If you touched her soul, there would be a deep sigh and you would know you were onto something. Such talent was opened up in those circles—it was astounding! Women like me. Women in worse states than mine. Women who had just run away from their husbands. Women in change of life. Women becoming lesbians. Women coming undone!

I walked into that first session in a near comatose state of mind—a stranger to myself on the edge of oblivion. We did a spontaneous writing; I remember my last line. "I am a dumb dog baying at the moon." But in that hour the writing pulled me like a magnet back into myself, and from that day the writing Muse never left my side. She was hippie-beautiful, wild, stoned, and a little crazy.

Months passed. A year passed. The writing grew. My children grew. I wrote at Winchell's Donuts, McDonald's, anywhere I could feel anonymous. Once, sitting in Denny's Diner, I had an imaginary affair with a handsome gray-haired man in a blue work shirt sitting across the room stealing glances at me. I sat there writing the poem, "Confession at Denny's"—lost track of time, got to Sami's daycare a half-hour late. She was the last child there, sitting forlorn, beside a fuming daycare worker with words for me.

I wrote on buses, in parks while the children played. I wrote on the backs of food stamp applications while sitting in line, on blank checks at the Village Laundry. At 3:00 in the morning while my family slept I clacked away on my typewriter, the Muse bouncing around the trailer like a crazed, trapped bird.

My life was saved.

I write while frying chicken
while tying shoes
a poem floats up out of the dirty dishes
I kick the legos aside
a poem is there
I take it on trips with me
pull it out when all else is unfamiliar
It keeps me company at night
wakes me up in the morning
It is my breakfast

And he, ironically, was the inspiration for all this writing. I was like Christine in *The Phantom of the Opera*, possessed by the phantom who infused in her the spirit to express herself in song..

I read my poetry at local coffee shops. I published a few when I felt like it. I listened to women's tales of liberation, poems about leaving—standing out on the road and hitchhiking to freedom. Women did it every day—just like that, they walked out the door, out of their marriages, putting one foot in front of the other. Did I really want to *be* one of those? I had no picture in my mind of how it would look, of what would come next. If only I had had a picture.

Leaving? It is more complicated than just walking out the door, says The White Raven. There must be an epiphany in leaving. Without that, there is only dullness of spirit, or fear of the unknown. This was the life I knew. My hold on him seemed so tenuous. And there were all those Other Women out there.

CHAPTER 14

Big Daddy Sun

ONE DAY THE COUNTY HEALTH inspector knocked on the trailer door, called in by old Mrs. Crawford's daughter across the street. He asked me what our sewage arrangements were and I stammered, "We're roughing it," which became another entry into the thick file of complaints at the county building department. Tom decided it was time to move to the top of the hill where there was a virginal septic tank waiting to be baptized.

The excavator who had carved our driveway hitched his tractor to the trailer. As the trailer was pulled away from its nesting place in the field I saw the dead grasses of the cesspool under its belly and wondered how we had survived all those months. I wanted to cry as I sat watching our home crawling, creeping up the hill and landing at the top with the broadside facing south.

It should have faced west so the trailer wasn't visible, like a gleaming tabernacle, to the world below. And anything facing south was a target for the afternoon sun. Big Daddy Sun. Fierce, blinding inferno, melting the sky as it rolled upward. Sizzling through clouds, it climbed its arc to the zenith of noon when the wheatgrasses popped and crackled and lizards came to the rocks to worship the Big Eye. Why I had come to hate the sun was not just my Russian blood. It was the trailer—seething metal box—that burned the sun into my psyche and scarred it, sun-shaped, forever.

Brother Sun, Sister Moon. St. Francis walked the earth and this he knew. The sun is male, no question of that—fiery, blazing star that you must never look at directly, for it may blind you. The sun's protective cloak of ozone is no doubt the work of the Mother. And now that the bad little Earth children have bungled things and blasted holes in the protective wrap, the sun is a threat to everyone, even the dark people deep in the jungles.

Soon, the ten thousand flies moved in. They had followed us up the hill. The trailer was their home too. I was no longer a shrieking woman pounding walls, as I was down below. I had given in. In a swoon, dreary and sullen, I knew that there would not be a drop of rain all summer. I dreamed of Midwest sudden thundershowers in a pink ozone sky and an iridescent green glow after the storm is spent. The sun. It got inside my head. It was a buzzing in my brain. This sun was making me insane.

Over the next year the trailer expanded. A room with a loft was added to the side facing the house. Tamar donated some of her white pickets and we put in a little fence between the trailer and the house, and grew some grass. Sami and Ben played on the deck of the house amidst the cement mixer and the timbers and the rebar and the concrete blocks—their playground, a construction zone.

Ben, now in first grade, ran down the hill each morning to catch his bus on Big Basin Way. Sami was almost three, and her infant screaming had turned to hollering. She had opinions now, and her need to be carried was never satisfied. Since the car would not make it up the driveway which kept going back to nature after the winter rains, I had to park at the bottom and carry up the groceries. Sami would stand at the bottom of the hill yelling, "Carry me, Mommy. Carry me!"

CHAPTER 15
All The Pretty Flowers

so easy
like a tooth extraction at the dentist
there were waiting rooms with magazines
tea and cookies afterward
it was so easy to pluck you
like a tiny alpine flower
out of the field of so many hundreds
there are so many pretty flowers
who would know?

When I got that queasy feeling I wanted to tell everyone. Secretly I ate crackers in the morning. We had planned our two. Who would figure that one might have plans for herself in that one week between the pill and the diaphragm. Tom wasn't happy about this. In fact, he tried to blame me, said he couldn't "get through another baby." He was, after all, a planner.

I looked for a loud sign to tell me what to do, hoped for obstacles that would make an abortion impossible, but when I called the clinic an easy voice informed me: "We have the procedures every Saturday. Don't eat breakfast. Bring your proof of pregnancy, and be prepared to pay the full amount in cash."

As we walked into the clinic, my family and I, everyone turned to stare. They were all young men nervously reading magazines, smoking cigarettes. A maternity ward waiting room scene like you see in the movies, except that these were boys.

"You go take the kids, I said, "and pick me up later."

In the back room, in a circle, sat the girls who went with the boys. It seemed that abortion for some of them was a new form of birth control. I volunteered to be first. Refused tranquilizers. Felt the needle in my cervix, heard the rattle of the machine that sucked the baby tissue by tissue into a tube and dropped it into a laboratory wastebasket.

Beds with colorful comforters. Attendants gliding from bed to bed like angels of mercy, checking blood pressure, serving tea and cookies. I wanted a chapel instead of a tea party.

In the waiting room, the nervous young men looked up from their magazines and watched me curiously as I walked toward the door. In the car, I kissed my children, and we wound through the mountains to home.

I was leaving for Toledo the next day. Tom watched me carefully all evening as I packed. At the departure gate we held each other, made promises. A new beginning. No more mistakes. And the rest was a dream.

First night of Hanukkah. Ben lighting candles with a *yamulke* on his head, repeating the Hebrew blessings after my father. Latkes, brisket. Log fire in the living room. Board games. Flickering candles and the smell of Mom's chocolate cake.

My sister Elaine and I dancing through Christmas-music stores trying on clothes. Walking home on a deep snow evening through the quiet of Old Orchard, I began to bleed. My legs chapped with cold blood, walking home.

Cocktail party. Everyone was there, everyone I ever knew. My old Hebrew teacher, my mother's Thursday night Mahjong club, cousins, aunts and uncles, and Dr. Singer who brought all six of us into the world. There was a bar. I drank too much.

The last night. Elaine and I went to Grandma Fanya's house to say good-bye. Once so large and heavy-breasted and jolly, she had lost her good health and had begun to shrink, each year a little more. That night she was very small and when I bent to hug her I feared that she might break.

We sat on the old blue sofa. Now that she was eighty-nine she was letting go, and the tales of her life as a Jewish girl in czarist Russia dropped from her as easily as Russian snow, and all the time she spoke she held my hand in her warm hand. Grandma said: "Do you know, my dears, how lucky you are that you grew up in a large family here in this country? Look at all six of you, how happy you are. Let me tell you a secret. A long time ago in Canada when I was struggling with four children and we had no money. . . I was so tired. We didn't have washers and dryers, you know. We did it all by hand. I found out I was going to have a fifth, and I thought *'I just can't do it.'* I went to our doctor and asked him, 'Is there anything I can do? I'm so tired. I have enough children.'"

"Well, the doctor had just returned from the hospital and he told me his patient had died. She was a woman who tried to get rid of her baby and she bled to death. The doctor looked me in the eye and said, 'Fanya Teitlebaum, you have four beautiful children and now you're going to have a fifth.' I rose even before he finished his sentence and said, 'I certainly am!' and ran out of the door and home to my children. And, my darlings, you know who was my fifth!" Of course we knew. It was our mother, Sophie.

"Go" she said to us. "Go have yourself big families and be mothers. Make more brothers and sisters. Zai gezundt!" She released my hand.

We rose, and at the door I kissed my shrinking Grandma good-bye and stepped outside into the frozen night.

I knew that sleep would not come to me, so I flipped on the TV by the round table in the kitchen, to fill my head with Johnny Carson, and made a cup of tea. The picture focused in on the story of a mature couple that finds they are pregnant. The woman, in her late thirties, is reluctant and wants to terminate the pregnancy but the man convinces her, takes her to La Maze classes, and then right there on NBC, I watched, dumbfounded, what should have been Johnny Carson but what was, instead, a baby being born.

I climbed the steps to my room, sat on the bed where Sami slept, and it was then that Superwoman of the clinic had her cry. I wept for the generations, for my grandmother and my mother, for their struggles and their gifts. For the world that had grown too small. For Sami, sweet blond hair swirled upon the pillow. And I wept for the baby who was pulled from her womb-deep sleep and bled into the snow.

CHAPTER 16

Curtains Orange and Pink

Is humanity in its adolescent stage? ponders The White Raven. The earth people are horny as a teenager. In 1973, Mother Earth came to her menses, began sloughing off the walls of Her great Collective Womb, at first a trickle, then a blood bath of babies, a tidal wave of blood.

After Roe v Wade they were handing out abortions like colorful rubbers, which was a bad thing for the Bible-thumping fundamentalists who defended life as yet unlived; a good thing for the liberated woman of Choice and for the planet whose children had multiplied quite enough; and a troublesome thing for the woman who was enough of a feminist to support Choice, and enough of a mother to suffer the ambiguity of knowing that mistakes can be made.

To make certain there would be no more mistakes, Tom had a vasectomy. It was not a Tom-like thing to do. He did not research it. He did not plan it. He did this for us, for me.

I am sitting on the floor staring at the flowers in the curtains.
They focus, defocus, meld together and glide apart—orange and pink flowers blatantly gay, twenty-nine cents a yard at Woolworths.

Baby Sam is pulling at me, crawling over me, kissing me, hitting me, yelling, "Cereal, Mommy! Cereal, Mommy!" I get up dizzy with the standing. She was playing with peach jam and mixing milk into a pan of tea leaves on the stove. I get her cereal, and go back to my floor place.

The phone rings: Mrs. Corn? This is Kaiser Hospital calling about your husband's sperm check. There is no sperm. He is clear.

I go to the bathroom
throw my diaphragm into the wastebasket
no more birth control
no more children
simple now
just sit here
watch them grow
flowers, orange and pink

PART 4

People of The Half-Built House

Do you think I know what I am doing?
that for one breath I belong to myself?
I know what I am doing
as much as a pen knows what it is writing
as much as a ball can guess where it is bouncing next

I am writing on blank checks at the Laundromat.
Why am I always writing poems
here between the washing and the drying
here with Sami on my lap, the radio blaring rock,
the rumbling of twenty electric dryers

Why am I not a tall lean Jewess
washing clothes on the banks
of the River Jordan?

Why am I here?
Why am I now?

CHAPTER 1

It is Fly Season Again

As I lay in bed dozing, I shooed away a face fly that kept eating at my eyes. A house fly flew under my skirt. A horse fly buzzed against the window at the end of the bed. It is fly season again. Insidious insects. I dread them more than rattlesnakes, more than scorpions. On the walls of our trailer hang old sketches of Tom from the San Francisco days, stained with tiny dots of fly dung.

With spring come the wildflowers, tiny delicate buds of purple, pink, blue, and gold sprinkled all down our hill—and with spring come the fly clouds to set up their summer home. Their holy shrine is our tiny trailer. We are the sacrificial offering.

Once, in the Childhood Land of Seasons, summers meant lightning bugs on muggy barbecue nights, soft chirping of crickets, butterflies, and June Bugs at Lake Erie. Mosquitoes were mosquitoes. Flies were flies. They seemed to have their place. Now I dread Fly Season as Kansas people dread tornadoes, as river people fear the raging storms. Soon our mobile home will be mobile with flies, and our fly rituals will begin.

In the cool mornings when they rest by the hundreds on the walls, the ceilings, in the curtain folds and on the plant leaves, Tom takes his special gray-white fly towel and walks up and down the trailer slamming them ten at a time. I follow after with a broom, sweeping them off the beds, the countertops, the floor and out the door. Then as the sun slowly warms the trailer, miraculously, hundreds more appear and begin their daily calisthenics, flying around in circles faster and faster as the degrees rise, and when the noon sun brings the temperature to one hundred, the air is noisy with them. If you look outside you see no flies. They are all inside our tiny home, doing their fly dance, mating in the air, mad with the heat.

Then in the evening as the air cools, they slow down and Tom, with his larger evening towel, starts at one end of the trailer flapping the huge towel up and down, herding the flies into the back room, slamming the sliding door shut so they're trapped. Then with much towel flapping, the flies explode en masse out the back door. Of course it's all useless, because the next day when someone opens the front door they'll all fly back in. It is their home too.

Of course there are flytraps. You will ask why don't we get flypaper? Yes, flypaper, to get caught in my hair, to get caught in Tom's mustache. A fly gets caught in it and slowly dies, buzzing in place, trying to free its legs. Our home, a flytrap with flytraps in it to trap flies.

Well, this is the last trailer summer. This is the year we'll finish our house. This is the year we will stand on one side of the trailer and push it off its piers and watch it crash down the hill rolling over and over into oblivion. This is the year.

We lasted one more year in the trailer. Old Mrs. Crawford's daughter and her husband across the street reported to the county that our trailer permit had expired one year ago. They were counting. (I'm glad somebody was.) We were called in by the district attorney who said it was illegal to live in the trailer anymore. Some folks up near Vajrapani wanted to buy it. The same excavator who once towed it up with a tractor returned with his tractor to drag it back down.

The family arrived. Melanie, the daughter, and Ben sat on the edge of the house observing. Ben sat very still watching the only house he could remember screech haltingly down the steep driveway toward the switchback.

"They're taking our house away. Where are we going to live now?"

"In the house model, Ben. We're going to live in the house model."

It was the edge of winter. Work had stopped. The money had run out. My father was in no position to lend another penny. He had stretched himself, and his ethics were strong and Jewish; he would not give to one what he could not give to all six children.

The first night in the house we slept on the floor. As the light faded I lay on the rug, with a strange feeling that something was moving toward me. Then I saw it—a gigantic black hairy tarantula crawling, ever larger, in my direction. This "house" of ours was just yesterday one part of a great meadow, and the tenants were the wild creatures creeping in and out of it as they pleased. We were "camping in" in their space. In that first week I saw a baby rattlesnake in the hallway, two more tarantulas, and scorpions in the garage.

I had read *The Findhorn Garden*, the story of the famous spiritual group that had come together in Scotland to collaborate with the nature spirits and create a garden community. They grew the most miraculous garden known to man. *The Findhorn Garden* taught that you could talk to the devas of the insects and animals, and if you spoke with respect and conviction, they would listen. I stood in the middle of the living room, cleared my throat and proclaimed:

"Okay, you bees and spiders, scorpions and snakes: I know this has been your territory, but now we are living here too. I have two small children who could get hurt. Please respect the boundaries of our home, and we will never harm you."

We never saw the tarantulas, snakes and scorpions again inside the house—only frogs, mice, snails, lizards, ants and naturally, hordes of flies. In summer the rattlers set up a nest under the platform in back of the house where Tom and I slept, but we always bagged them and carried them away. No creature was ever hurt. We kept our bargain, and they kept theirs.

One Sunday at the flea market Tom discovered a man selling large rolls of mylar. He bought them all. Winter was on its way, and once again the oak floorboards had to be protected from the rains. Mylar was secured across the rounded floors of the kitchen and living room which had no walls or ceilings. Corrugated fiberglass siding was nailed to the vertical posts around the entire house, and then more mylar attached to the siding. The house was wrapped like a mummy in plastic.

Some folks from Vajrapani came to see our house. They wanted mylar too. The next Sunday they rushed to the flea market and the man was there again with an endless supply of rolls. They bought them all, and soon it was mylar city in the Buddhist backwoods of Boulder Creek.

The ceiling in our living area was bridge timbers, bought in an auction, that would be the floorboards of the second floor. There was no roof. No doors. The windows were mylar. Electricity came from the temporary power pole near the house. The stairs from the garage below led up to our living space, with a small landing at the top. A Wedgewood cook stove was hooked up to a five-gallon propane tank. One toilet sat naked and exposed in the back room where Tom and I slept. The salvaged claw foot bathtub sat in the hallway. There was a hot water heater, but it wasn't connected to anything. I still had to heat water on the stove. I used to promise myself that if I just had hot water, I would not ask for anything, ever again.

Settling into the house, I did what women do: sprinkled pillows here and there, made curtains to cover shelves of food and mice droppings. Life was easier than it had been down below in the field. The children were fine. We had a toilet. The toilet was hooked up to the septic tank. A miracle. We had a view of the mountains. We had space. Tom and I even managed to fall in love again. We were good at that.

Tom, who had become a first-class scrounger, a pillager of waste, had found in San Jose a carpet place that threw old office rugs into the dumpster out back. He took them all. For the internal walls, we put up the salvaged rugs. My favorite was the green one separating the kitchen area from the landing at the top of the steps.

Tom had gotten good at building shelves. If anyone could build a shelf, it was Tom. There were shelves in the makeshift kitchen above the stove, and by Ben's bed, an eight-foot wall of shelves where he kept his Tonka trucks and his legos.

The depressed lioness was sprung from her eight-foot-wide cage, and she settled into her new lair—the Half-Built House.

I am your sweet soul love baby lady girl
and when I am in our bed
then I am home

CHAPTER 2

Mother, Mommy, Mom

My parents were coming to visit. They had heard that we were living in the house now. Tom made excuses to be gone. I made lists:

debris pile to the dump
pretty curtains to hide the shelves of old food
throw out moldy rugs
put all the naily lumber into one neat pile
cover it

When you look at a list you made twenty years ago, you see a snapshop of your life back then.

Tamar and Charles came from Omland to help—Tamar in her lavender overalls rolled up and a blue bandanna, Charles in a Hawaiian straw hat and white shirt with crocheted flowers. It was ninety degrees.

"Do you want to smoke a joint?" Charles offered. He rolled a fat one. We ate crackers and cottage cheese, getting high on Maui Wowie. I put on Joan Baez and we danced around, sweeping and scrubbing.

I danced onto the deck (the future living room without walls), and yelled through the music, "Are we hippies?"

"What?"

"Are we hippies?"

"Of course," laughed Tamar.

Charles approached me, rubbed his beard, fixed those cosmic blue eyes on mine and said: "We are Aquarian people. We are making the world ready for the New Age. We are the grandparents of the children of the Age of Aquarius." I was hippie-happy then.

My mother followed my father up the dusty driveway, trudging slowly, slowly to the top. She sat collecting herself on the old brown sofa, shooing away the flies.

Yesterday we had scrubbed the house, dancing and dusting, stoned and happy. The half-built house was far better than the filthy trailer down in the field, the first time they had visited. But without her saying a word, I could see that to my mother's eyes my home was squalor and degradation. It was hard for me to know anymore.

Walking down the graveled drive,
her hand riveted to Dad's shoulder for fear of falling,
Mom said to me:
"Why don't you sell it, sell your land, do something else?
You're not getting any younger."
Mother, Mommy, Mom. . .
I have walked on mountain ridges with a baby in my belly.
I have birthed a child by candlelight.
I have learned to live in this
Aquarian counterculture world. . .

Weren't we just earth people, land pioneers? A part of history?

I wasn't ever sure.

CHAPTER 3

Homesteaders

We are the people
who squat on land
who do not take out loans to pay contractors
to build wooden frame houses
We are the people of the half-built house
held together by plastic, fiberglass, and rugs

Here on this naked hill we live
no trees to hide us
They call us hippies, drop-outs, dead-beats
and they think we do it to spite them
to be different

We are trying to build a house

I HAD THIS LIFE-LONG ANTIPATHY to intense light, to hot sun and boring blue skies without a cloud; I had a craving for rain, fog, sleet, hail and snow—in other words, weather. The gloaming was mine—that magical space just before dark, and the velvet of night when everything looks altered and secretive.

In the childhood Land of Seasons, you could be dropped anywhere into the cycle and know by the smell and the light and the air what month it was: the lilac breath of spring, the dense, soft, luscious summer heat; the sun-crisp, leaf-burning autumn cold that smelled of winter, that laid a white carpet over the dead crunch of leaves, from which the first spring crocus poked its head. It was like a ballet.

In the Time Warp of the Half Built House, summer and winter landed like the swing of a pendulum, heavy and extreme and definite, without much in between. The drone of heat vaporizing the rains; the rains returning again to drown out the sun. It was like a battle.

And so again the pendulum swing of winter hit and our driveway, leading uphill like a pilgrim's path to the plastic acropolis at the top—this driveway, carved and crevassed with run-off from the rains, returned to nature. It refused to stay a driveway. The thistles grew taller and more stately each year, like flags staked there by Mother Nature to announce that She was winning. They grew like a curtain around the pile of debris, as if to say, "The more you put here, the thicker we will grow." Thistle bushes seven feet high with sticker claws and purple prickly flowers. They were the healthiest, hardiest plants I have ever seen.

I didn't mind that nature was winning. I wasn't trying to win anything. I only wanted a bit of comfort for my kids, for Tom and me. I wanted normalcy. I wanted a peaceful country scene. I wanted to live in the Comfort Zone. I wanted in.

The house was immobilized, bound and bandaged in plastic—a house in bondage. The status quo had sunk into the floorboards, into the faux walls, into the whole abandoned soul of the house. The few fruit trees Tom had planted struggled along. A scattering of small, puckered peaches hung from a tree down the hill.

Winter came hard. The sound of pounding rain that is delicious when you are warm and cozy and dry by the evening fire was, for us, a prelude to a frantic scene with pails and mops and rags. Tom was anxious and argumentative and dejected because he knew that this was all his doing, and he wanted to find some way to blame me, but he couldn't, so he just kept busy running around with buckets and laying plastic on top of plastic. The oak flooring of the future living room was already warping, with squeaks and soft spots.

We had visitors one day— his sister and mother from Los Angeles, and Tom's Grandma Corn who had money and a luxury apartment in Florida. Grandma Corn wanted to see for herself this famous grandiose house her grandson was building.

They parked their car at the base of the hill toward sundown, and we shuttled them up in the broken-down VW bug that could take the weathered road better. Grandma Corn climbed the stairs leading to the makeshift living area, walked from the open living room deck, through the hallway, past the future dining room—walked through room after room in silence, and then proclaimed: "It's awfully big. Why does it have so many rooms? You know, you can only be in one room at a time." Just then a bat flew through the house.

To anyone down below this looked like a ruin, an old abandoned wreck of a house. To our friends and the Buddhists in the woods, we were fellow homesteaders all in various stages of building. The Santa Cruz Building Department, though they knew of the backwoods projects, chose to keep one eye shut. They were busy enough with all the million-dollar homes for the techies who worked in Silicon Valley, bent on turning Boulder Creek into a bedroom community.

The chief building inspector liked us. He was a fatherly man with a sense of humor. He made suggestions. He would have done anything possible to help the project along. He labeled our file The Carpet House.

Why did it have so many rooms? asks The White Raven. Perhaps to house Tom's inflated psyche. Whose house was this, anyway? At the one tiny moment of conception when I sketched the rounded Welsh house, it took on a feminine aspect. Then he ran with the design, poured his seed into it, drowned it in testosterone, and from that moment on, I stepped quietly back, making curtains and putting up pictures on the rug walls.

This was not my house; I did not need a castle.

CHAPTER 4

But With Love. . .

A WAD OF TOILET PAPER FOR MY BIRTHDAY

(WUI— Written Under the Influence——Shrooming)

It is my birthday. Alexandra called yesterday to ask what was my favorite cake. She really likes me. And so I have carved out this day for myself. My children are at Alexandra's. They spent the night there, went bumping off in the back of a truck yesterday. I miss them now. Their faces are so bright. They love me. This is my day.

It was a troubled night. . . went to bed with the nightmare of this scene. How would we ever get our house done if Tom smoked pot around the clock? When he smokes he only wants to do the fun projects. He's been milling up old redwood logs down the hill for days now. Yesterday he milled up a bay laurel burl. He was so excited at each cut. He couldn't stop until the whole thing was sliced up, like light rye at the delicatessen. He enjoys himself. Now, from the garage I hear the back and forth of sand paper. He's sanding out translucent surfaces in bay laurel, trippin' on birdseye.

So I wake up after a crazed night, thinking we will drift on like this forever because what will one day make him all of a sudden want to get serious and go up on the house with the one-hundred-dollar calculator and start figuring out the iron brackets and all the angles that are going to make this house come together.

I wake up thinking that the first thing I'm going to see in my day is Tom's stony face. . . that morning stony grin. I turn to look and there it is, the grin, and I sniff the marijuana in the air. My plan for the day was to eat a Psilocybin mushroom I have been saving for a special day. Another time Tom and I ate them together, and we laughed at our crazy scene on the hill. We walked to Alexandra's house, and on the way down the hill we surveyed the tires, the bricks, toilets, wire. . . all the treasures buried in the tall grasses. Tom said, "Was this all here when we moved in? I don't remember it. There must be a crazy person living here. Where'd all this stuff come from?" We laughed and laughed.

He turned to me and said, with his stony face, "Do you want your mushroom now? "No," I said, "I have to meditate first." So I meditated, then ate my mushroom for breakfast. It tasted foul, but I chewed it up and swallowed it, took the phone off the hook and crawled back into bed.

I was so sick. I was eighty-five years old and dying. There were screams outside the window from across the field. I was an old lady dying in a hospital room. It was familiar. I had been there before. The taste of death was in my mouth, and a slow pounding in my throat.

"It'll pass," Tom said. "It won't last long." I waited, dying, staring at the knots in the pinewood. I watched breasts rippling out of the walls, breasts into breasts into breasts. Suddenly I knew I had to get up, get outside. I didn't want to die on my birthday.

I walked on rubber legs. What were all these things all over the floor? An old dirty piece of cushion foam, clothes, sewing things, a curtain rod. Why is it always such a mess here? Why wasn't I stepping out of my queen bed with a Macy's quilt, into my master bedroom with a grand piano by the window and Persian rug, and brownstone fireplace with plants hanging all around?

My eyes stuck to the floor, filthy—full of dead plant leaves and yesterday's dirt. Smell of garbage. The rug, I have to throw it out. It's dirty beyond cleaning. I'll throw it out like all the others and get a new one.

I started to cry. Everything was so ugly. I went outside and next to the garage was a pile of junk, trash, garbage, the next trip to the dump. . . when the truck gets fixed. I saw it all and it hurt my eyes. What people can do to a hill. It was just a green hill when we got here. I looked around at the broken toys and funky chairs and the banged up dirty cars and it all hurt my eyes. "I don't see," I cried. "I am here in it so long, I stopped seeing it anymore." I turned from the trailer scene and looked out down the hill where green and yellow grasses waved in the breeze. "I want to sit in the grass," I said. "Tom, I sobbed, "It's not funny this time. I don't want to laugh. I only want to cry."

"Then cry," he said.

So I cried and cried, and from the pocket of my grey coat I pulled out an old frazzled paper napkin to blow my nose. "Tom, for my birthday, please. . . I need some clean toilet paper to blow my nose." He got up and brought me a big wad which I stuffed into my torn pocket. This grey coat, the one I bought in Toledo when I visited my family in the winter—a seventy-dollar suburban coat with fake fur collar and belted waist. It's all ripped inside. It's no good. I can't even wear a good coat anymore. In Boulder Creek it tears to shreds.

I cried great wells of tears. I cried for my soiled torn seventy-dollar coat from Toledo. I cried for the ugliness. I cried for my dirty children, for the pretty square cars and neat houses in suburbia, for my parents in their formal dining room and my father who listens to Brahms with headphones on when he comes home from the office. I cried for my mother who waits to hear from us, who waits for my father to take the headphones off and come to dinner. I cried for the Jesus freaks next door.

My hands fell on Tom's hands. I never really saw how scarred and bruised and cut up they were. I held them and cried for Tom's hands and for his tennis shoes that are held together by broken laces and duct tape. I cried for our house with its ripply rain-warped floorboards and its stairway that goes half way up and stops in the air.

I cried for everything. . . and as my compassion expanded, the ugliness began to dissipate like morning fog. "It's just a scene," I laughed, "different from most people's, but is it really worse than gas stations and Cadillacs and McDonald's? Why does suburbia seem more right? Just because it hangs together in neat squares and angles and because garbage cans are hidden underground, and cars are tucked away behind magic genie garage doors?

"It's such a pretty hill," I said. "I just want to make it pretty again." I looked into his eyes and kissed his torn-up hands and said, "I just want to be with you." He said, "When you're looking at someone, you don't have to see the things around you."

"You should be a poet," I said. "Have you ever written anything?"

"No" he laughed.

"Will you write me something sometime, please? Just a postcard?"

"Sometime," he said.

We sat down on the chairs outside the trailer and I cried some more. "Tom, we don't have to finish this house, you know. We could sell the land and go somewhere else. Is your heart really in it?"

He leaned back in the chair and said softly and with tenderness: "I do care, and I want to finish it. I've been working on the calculations. I know you feel helpless, but don't worry. We'll get out of this dump. The house will go up fast now. The hardest part is over."

I cried and cried. It's what I wanted to hear, because if his heart wasn't in it there was no way we could finish a house like this. But with love, it could be built.

We took a walk up Big Basin Road. A butterfly by the roadside struggled to move. I picked it up. Its wing was wounded and it tried to flutter away. "Now it's scared," I said. "It's struggling because I picked it up." Tom took it from me, put it down and said, " Its struggle is that it's dying." I cried for the butterfly.

We noticed delicate lavender wildflowers growing along the road, and wondered if we could grow them on our hillside. When we returned home we found them growing profusely at the bottom of the hill. At home on the table was a chocolate cake that said in red icing: HAPPY BIRTHDAY, and a bottle of Pepsi and a birthday napkin. Alexandra had done this for me. Alexandra loves me. I am loved. Yes, and Tom loves me. There is tenderness in him.

Tom has been working the rest of the day on the calculations. His notebook is filling up with technical pictures and notations. Each bracket is numbered and there is an index on the first page that tells where every bracket goes. And he is doing it stoned. Suddenly I come to realize what I have always known, that he can do anything stoned. He works well stoned because when he's stoned he doesn't worry or feel the burden of what he's doing. I resolve that I won't worry anymore about his not worrying. He said with tears that his heart is in this house, that he really wants to finish it, and I believe him. I do believe him.

As I believe that one day the trailer will be rolled away unveiling a majestic mountain home built of handsome redwood timbers and windows all around its rounded rooms. There will be lilac bushes surrounding the house and apple trees budding up and down the hill. The unruly stacks of scrap wood will be gone uncovering a driveway that leads into a garage where cars are parked. And gone, gone will be the tires and the rusty nails and the garbage cans and broken toilets, and in their place, grass will grow. The redwood slabs that sit like mammoth wood sculptures on the sides of our driveway will be redwood tables inside our house and window seats and spice shelves and we will come in on winter evenings and build a fire in the living room. . .

and sit on the slate floor's thick white rug
and listen to Mendelsohn's Fourth
gushing from giant speakers
built into the wall. .

CHAPTER 5

Grandma Fanya

AS THE THIRD SUMMER PEAKED, once again the towering thistles grew brittle and their purple flowers blew away. But not the pile of rubbish next to the house. That ageless pile seemed to have a life of its own, festering and growing: old rotten wood, rusted chimney pipes, torn mylar, mildewed books ruined from winter damp, boxes of rusty nails, bags of cement solidified by the rains. This pile was the first thing I saw on coming up the driveway, the first thing I saw in leaving the house. I wanted to bomb it, vaporize it.

I had been sleeping far too many hours in the day. I only wanted to sleep. The heat droned on as one day melted into another, and I moved as in a dream, feeding my children, wiping their faces, putting food on the table, clearing it off.

At the far end of the house where the naked toilet sat was our bed. On a table at the foot of the bed sat an old black and white TV. When it was on, every few minutes the picture would begin to roll. I lay there, flanked by Sami and Ben. In my hand was a stick, and when the picture rolled I would hit the TV with the stick. I lay on the bed watching a movie in the heat of the afternoon sun—drifting in and out of consciousness.

Suddenly I bolted, sat straight up, as if someone had struck *me* with a stick. In the air were the words, "You're going to be dead someday." I sat there blinking and could still hear the voice and those words, hanging there in the fetid air.

In those days Tamar sang and played guitar to local children's groups in the Valley. One day she came to visit after singing at the Boulder Creek recreation hall. Her thick hair exploded from the kerchief on her head. She had a long flowered dress and sandals. She sat down on the edge of the bed and placed her guitar against the wall.

"Do you believe we have spirit guides who talk to us?" I asked.

"Yes, I do. I know mine was there the day I met Charles in Big Sur. Sometimes it's more obvious than others."

"I have one who never appears unless I'm in dire straights, unless I'm about to die. I heard his voice the other day. It said: 'You're going to be dead someday.' I wouldn't mind a more personal, intimate angel. I used to think I had a purpose, that I was meant to be an artist or a poet. It's why I moved out to California in the first place. Other people seem to have spirit guides. Look at Karen. She gets pulled here to be a midwife and within months she is catching babies for all the Buddhist families at Vajrapani. She told me she is guided every step of the birthing. And you, you are teaching songs to children. It's your work. As for me, I can't see over the garbage pile. All I can think about is getting hot water. I would kneel down and worship the hot water heater if only it would work! I think my spirit guide is a fat capitalist with a cigar in his mouth who enjoys seeing hippies suffer."

"Then fire him." said Tamar. "Get another one. Send him on his way. Ask for a wise woman, a strong, smart woman in a long dress."

Trips to Toledo became a sort of pilgrimage to the holy land, a place of normalcy where, according to Sami, Grandma Sophie, my mother, had a laundromat inside her house. We always went in winter because I wanted Sami and Ben to walk in snow. I wanted their Russian blood to come alive in a land where it wasn't Disney green all year. But Sami would bury her face in my coat and beg to go back inside.

Ben and I walked through the snowy streets of Old Orchard, through the parking lot of B'nai Israel Synagogue to Darlington Home for the Jewish aged where Grandma Fanya Teitlebaum lay. Her heart was failing.

As I stood by her side, she drifted in and out of Russian, her swollen legs weighting her like ballasts to the bed. When she drifted in, she focused on me and said, "My darling, I am ready to face death. Tell your mother and Aunt Ruth to let me go."

I gave her water, helped make her more comfortable, sat with her while she hovered between the old world, this world, and the next. I kissed her goodbye and she went off mumbling in Russian again. As Ben and I walked back to Drummond Road he asked, "Is your Grandma going to be the next one there to die?"

"I think that maybe she is."

Sami sat looking at her doll that had small breasts
and said, "My doll is a woman"

"Like you," I said
"No, I'm a girl," she laughed
"But inside you there is a woman
She just hasn't come out yet"

She looked up at me with big eyes. . .
And one day she will look down at me
as I lie in my bed
She will take a brush and brush my silver hair
and she will feed me with a spoon

CHAPTER 6

Anniversary March

I WOKE UP ONE MORNING, looked around, and it suddenly dawned on me that we were living in a deserted construction zone. The money was gone. The Beautiful Men from Maine were busy on their own project—converting their communal barn into a two-story house that would be bought by Vajrapani for visiting teachers and guests. From barn to commune to Buddhist house. In those times even a barn could have a spiritual evolution.

A deserted construction zone? And what of our marriage: That too was deserted, left back in San Francisco, there between the speakers in the Zone Called Paradise. We had just careened haphazardly out of the Zone and somehow landed at the top of a hill with two small children in a gigantic half-built fortress.

I remembered when Tom suggested that we might have to move into our house before the cabinets were done. *Live without cupboards, without cabinets and drawers?* I thought. *I don't know. I don't know.* And I magnanimously agreed to that sacrifice. To think how far I must have evolved since then.

I want a plushy rug your feet sink into
when you take your shoes off
I want wooden cabinets, fluffy velvet pillows
and a brass lamp over the dining room table
I am a neurotic poor lady wringing her hands

Seven Year Anniversary Letter from Toledo

We used to have a marriage, our anniversaries an occasion for champagne, the way our wedding was—all those bottles of Korbel bubbling in the San Francisco of our Love.

Tonight I want to look at us as an old friend whom I haven't seen in seven years. Our wedding picture is on my mother's wall. I have taken it off and I am devouring every detail:

> *the tan bricks of the fireplace, charred around the opening from evening fires. There are vases of red, pink, and white carnations bought by my father, that sit on the mantel, flanking the menorah, a wedding gift from my Rabbi boss. The mirror above the mantel glows with the flash of this picture. The reflection of the living room crystal chandelier peeks through the flowers. We sit on a gold satin pillow on the red shag rug that camouflages your red socks. You wear corduroy pants and a white turtleneck shirt that I bought you for the wedding. There is a clock behind you. It is 7:05. I am sitting next to you in my purple, gold and green satin wedding gown with the frivolous bead bodice, the dress I bought in Ann Arbor on a lark, knowing we would marry one day. My shoulders are white and soft. My face is glowing. White pearl earrings. My bosom is full. I am smiling and so full of beauty.*

I get up and walk towards the bathroom, catch my breath from the pain in my leg. I limp into the bathroom and flip on the light. I stand at the mirror and I am crying. It is not just for the face in the mirror that I am crying. It is for this:

> *The red shag rug lies trapped and mildewed under a pile of bricks at the bottom of the hill. The green love pillow is squashed like a sausage into a sofa frame. The menorah has been thrown out. The gold satin pillow reeks with stale pee. The wedding dress is stuffed into a plastic bag. The bead bodice was cut into a Halloween mask and lost somewhere. Your gold corduroy wedding pants were dropped into a free box at the flea market.*

We know how to destroy, you and I. But those are just things. What of us? How do you look at a marriage in a mirror? This marriage limps along as I do. I am no longer brave. I am no longer superwoman. I am sick. I have seen it in the mirror.

I am in Toledo now where I was a young girl once, where I flit from shopping center to shopping center searching for something I have left behind, for something I need. I want to turn our hill upside down, sell out and go to France with you, tear up that scene that hangs together like a sick collage. And yet: I know that as sure as the moon and sun will trade places in the sky these next ten days, I will gather up bristle blocks and legos, search for lost socks, pack my bags. We will drive to Toledo Airport through the snow and board the plane, leaving my tearful mother at the gate. There will be lunch on the plane. The children will be restless.

I will wear my soft blue jeans and red turtleneck shirt and I'll see you standing there in your brown down jacket and your grin. We will hug and we will kiss. You will stoop down, embrace your children, tousle Ben's hair.

We will drive home in our beat up VW and I will wish that I had cleaned it before I left. We will head up our driveway and I will try not to let it all in at once. I will turn my head from the rubbish pile, snub the cracked sink by the garage, ignore the clutter by the steps, and I know that once inside, once I have accepted the rusty toilet, the dirty brown rug, the dying plant between the speakers, that once the children are finally in bed, we will come together hungry for the touch. We know how to love, you and I.

In my leg burns a searing, rushing, scarlet
cord of pain

I carry it all with me
all, baby

like a ball and chain
drag it through the day
pull it into bed with me at night

Our marriage staggers on
sustains itself
like a mammoth dinosaur
eating leaves

Our marriage marches on
I am limping after it

CHAPTER 7

Birthday

Your hips are out
You have an acute muscle spasm
In your lower spine
Go to bed

I drive home a cripple
wondering who will watch my children
when he is at work
and will I need a bedpan?

Slow shuffle steps
I stand between my bed and the kitchen sink
staring at last night's dishes

I am so old and it's only morning

THE PAIN OF DEMOLITION AND hauling and carrying babies had clamped like a straightjacket onto my hips. There were times when I couldn't bend at all, and being careful dancing was the antithesis of hippie freedom. When I rose from sitting, a rushing pain of fire tore into my leg. My face was drained and pale. I couldn't eat.

Boulder Creek was a magnet for new age techniques and healing centers. A group called the Neuropsychics came together. They met each Sunday in the White House at the south end of town where spiritual healings were held. They dressed in white and sang in a cacophony of strange chanting, while walking around the room embracing and kissing one another.

On weekdays the healers had a clinic in the White House and the locals came. Their healing practices were delivered directly from the spirit world through automatic writings.

The healing methodology was based on the belief that virtually all physical ailments come from negative thought processes and deviation from your inner truth. When you lay face down, they gave you a truth test. They asked you something like your name or where you live. Immediately upon answering, they stimulated a point in your upper back and then touched the sensitive area in back of your knees. When a truthful answer was given, the healer would feel a simultaneous neuron sensation behind both knees. If there was negativity or untruth, this response would be blocked. In this way they identified negative thinking that created pain and sickness.

I was taken into a small room with a man named David. He was from New York. We soon discovered that the pain in my leg was—no surprise—about the abortion.

"It's been almost nine months now, I said to David. "I would have birthed her about now. I can't undo what I have done. There is no way out of this."

"When you aborted the baby, do you believe it had a soul already?"

"Yes."

"If it had a soul, then you have a spirit baby. You can talk to her. You can sing to her, ask for her forgiveness. I'm going to leave you alone in here now and I want you to talk to your baby. I'll be back in fifteen minutes."

When David entered the room, he said, "Man, it's hot in here. Do you feel that heat? You've whipped up quite a lot of energy here." He was right. The room was warm; I was on fire.

I have never known if David was a true healer. He was glib, intelligent, perceptive, and sincere. The Neuropsychics are long gone now, the followers dispersed. David became a salesman for Nexxus beauty products. His wife is a computer programmer. All I know is that what he did worked. He gave me options when I had been stuck in the belief that there were no options. The girdle of pain slowly melted away.

And I came to know that a spirit baby lived on our hill. Call me hippie. Call me California. Call me tra-la-la. But I know what I know. There was a spirit baby on the hill. Sometimes I would sit on the slope below the half-built house, the sun bleeding into the Santa Cruz mountains, and I would know she was there, wood spirit of the treetop branches, brushing the wheatgrasses, her touch as soft as a whisper. I would talk to her, sing to her, wondering who she was and what she would have become. I will always be her mother. I will always wonder.

a rhythmic throbbing in my womb
haunted me all the week
you remembered what you were supposed to do
and in the still of night
I birthed you upside down
in a dream
Oh Rock a bye baby
Happy birthday to you

CHAPTER 8

The Proposition

MICHAEL LUCKIE WAS CO-MANAGING A desktop publishing business in Oakland with his mate, Chris. At his invitation I drove up there one day to have lunch. He said he had something important to ask me.

Michael was mustached and looked dashing. He had had surgery the previous year to reconstruct his receding chin. He could not tolerate the thought of growing older without some improvements. Over lunch at a local Chinese restaurant, he began:

"I want to ask you something. Please don't answer until you hear it all. I have always thought so highly of you. You and Tom were my best friends in the Berkeley days. I'm happy enough with Chris and the business is doing well, but it isn't enough. I want to father a child. And you are the only woman I would consider. You are healthy, intelligent, from good Russian stock (he blurted out a laugh). I would take complete care of the child. You would only have to carry him."

This seemed an absurd idea, and yet at the same time so touching, almost alluring. I nearly cried. "Your timing could not be stranger. I am just now beginning to get over the guilt of an abortion I had last year." Luckie's face went blank. He didn't want to know more. He simply offered: "Well, this sounds preposterous, but maybe this will absolve you of your guilt, give you the opportunity to make it right."

"You sure know which buttons to push, don't you? You know how I love being pregnant and giving birth. In a way, it doesn't seem that far-fetched to me, but to tell the truth, I don't see how I could not be with the baby afterward. I've never understood how that works. I'm sure it wouldn't work for me."

"I knew you'd say that. I just felt I had to ask. You were the only one I would ask, and I owed it to myself to try."

I loved Mike for asking me. Driving home, I felt a sense of well-being sweep over me. He reminded me that I was a good person.

The last time I saw Luckie was months later when he came to visit us in the half-built house. He parked his low riding Citroen at the bottom, and walked up. He stayed for dinner, and after returning from the naked toilet at the end of the hall in the bathroom without walls, he scolded us.

"The toilet doesn't flush. It's barbaric for a person to have to leave his feces in someone's home."

He hurried down the hill to his Citroen, never to be seen again.

It was no surprise that he later died of AIDS, in light of the multitude of bathhouses he had frequented in the 60s. Luckie, one of the dearest, saddest people I was lucky enough to know.

CHAPTER 9

Wheatgrass Hill

NEVER THINK THAT JUST BECAUSE I was crazy some of the time, and there was no heat in winter or walls or a ceiling, that my kids were miserable. We would go to movies, to the playground, to the Boardwalk, to Fosters Freeze for fries while the clothes tumbled in the dryer at the Village Laundry. Ben and Sami were among the many counterculture kids who had strange lifestyles.

In summer the tall wheatgrasses of the hill turned blond—and when the sun sank into the distant mountains, the deep wet colors would jump out of the grasses at the threshold of twilight. It was our yearly tradition that we would choose a summer evening to be "wheatgrass day." Sami would choose a special dress, and she and Ben would scamper around on the hill among the tall grasses, and I would take photos—quality photos with the Nikon F—as they played. Today there is a wheatgrass album, every year showing them older and every year revealing a different mood. There are photos from one year when Sami looks like a little Amish girl in her brown lacy dress, and she has a soft, sad, thoughtful gaze in every single photo.

Ben surrounded himself at night with a menagerie of stuffed animals, his favorite being his long red snake called Sparkle, for the jeweled eyes

I had sewn on. Sami had a doll with a wobbly rubber head. We would go to Roaring Camp, home of the big steam train in Felton, where we'd have a picnic and walk around the duck pond. Once Sami was carrying her doll piggy back, holding onto the legs, and as she walked along the doll's head fell off. She kept on walking unaware of her headless child. It is a poignant picture in my mind, both funny and full of pathos.

On Sami's birthdays I was always a nervous wreck. She, being a girl, was aware of the social norms, and I tried, as a poor helter-skelter mom, to accommodate. I made parties with balloons and favors. Once I even managed a skating rink party. But for the gifts, I secretly shopped at the Boulder Creek Thriftshop and wrapped the pretty shirts and sweaters and necklaces in tissue paper and boxes so they all looked new. But she knew. She knew everything. She must have known, because as she grew older, if she and I were in town and I started veering toward the thriftshop as if it were Saks Fifth Avenue, she would grab my hand like a stern grandmother, and pull me away from the force field of the thriftshop.

Despite the guilt that colored my motherhood, I know my kids respected me and were paying attention to my all-night clacking on the typewriter. They saw my work from life drawing sessions. One Mothers Day I got the best gift ever. It wasn't flowers. It wasn't a scarf or jewelry or perfume. It was a ream of typing paper and a box of pastels.

CHAPTER 10

Center Post III

Red clouds smoke up before the rising moon
There is drama in the sky
I am angry

You are sunk deep in a thick ring of dreams
I am the crazy lady of the night
and will I make it through another summer?

I'm not the same sweet soul baby lady girl
I was when you met me
and it ain't gonna be pretty around here

It ain't gonna be pretty

THERE WERE BUDDHISTS IN THE backwoods and healers and holy places and holy people. There were also nut jobs.

Bernie had charisma. He drew people like blood draws flies. He was tall and lean with thick dark hair, intensely bright eyes that bored into your brain and made you feel he was reading your every thought.

He bought land cheap, the parcel before the bend in the road that led to Vajrapani. A dip in the road and you crossed the bridge into Bernie land. While he worked on building his square house, he and Linda, his small blond nurse lover, lived in a tiny trailer. At the entrance to the trailer was a birdcage with a large parrot named George. Surrounding the trailer was a menagerie of animals: German Shepherds, horses, geese, chickens, guinea hens and a few pigs. There in the woods they lived like outlaws.

In the real world he had been an artist and a successful ad man. In the woods he applied his genius to survival and spoofing the establishment. He wrote articles in newspapers proclaiming his road to salvation and signed them "The Mother." As a church, his square house in the middle of nowhere would be tax-free. His religion attracted an odd assortment of misfits who joined his church through correspondence and who got healing advice from this austere "priestess" who had given up everything to live in the woods.

For Tom, the problems of house and marriage and kids vanished on the dirt road to Bernie's. It was like the good old boys club of the backwoods. They both had brilliant minds, loved pot, and they talked stony-talk far into the night.

Bernie was sexy, and had he been a cult leader, he might have had a string of concubines winding through the woods to his trailer door. I must admit that I was turned on by him, yet wary of his power. Mostly, I stayed away, and in the evenings, waited for the whirring sound of Tom's VW to signal he was home.

Tom was at Bernie's when I read the note he left for me on the redwood table.

> The reason we are closer now is that three years ago
> I had an affair. I was at the bottom of my life.

It helped me come back to you. I couldn't tell you then because you were not strong enough. . .
It was to protect you. I love you more than ever.

Tom

I read this over and over, my heart pounding and my head spinning. I scribbled my reply below his note:

Before dinner? You leave me with the children and tell me this before dinner?

Her name was Justine. Remember our trip to Tassajara, the Zen retreat? He had met her there in the rapids while I was nursing Sami, envying the naked bodies draped over boulders in the river. She was the reason he was curiously energetic that night in our cabin. She was the angel of mercy who pulled him up from the "bottom of his life" and made him feel good about himself. It's lucky for him that he didn't tell me then. I might have been after him with a butcher knife.

For two weeks I didn't sleep. I was the crazy lady of the night. For him this happened three years ago and it was done. For me it happened yesterday, and I would not be done until I went back to that place three years before when the trailer was in the field down below, and I was insane with flies and the stinking cesspool—back to the days when I was a screaming lunatic, pounding walls. I would not be done until I knew every detail.

He thought that I would understand, now that I was strong and we were close again. But my anger was strong too—fresh, bright, healthy, relentless. It wasn't just about his deceit. It was about all the unnecessary hardship of the past four years—the lack of hot water and plumbing, the cold winters without walls, our neglected children. And I became obsessed—torturing him, interrogating him, finding out when and how he got to her home in Berkeley, imagining what they were doing together when I was heating water on the stove for baths.

Hate is in the details.

Here is the story of a twelve-by-twelve, twenty-two-foot-long timber—the center post of our home: 1) Tom and I on a journey north to Elmer's Downieville mill when I was pregnant, to reserve it; 2) the crash of the timber as it was being winched into place, nearly smashing me and infant Sami; 3) and now this: his confession that he went on a joy ride with HER to Downieville to retrieve the timber and bring it home, and that they had slept in OUR double-mummy red down sleeping bag. This "detail" put me over the edge, into an adrenaline-fueled fury of sleepless nights.

A gigantic piece of wood redolent first with hope, then near disaster, and now the markings of sexual deceit.

I wondered what Elmer and his wife must have thought when Tom and Justine came driving up their driveway in a two-ton truck. They must have looked at each other wondering what happened to that nice pregnant wife he was with last time—and who is this new woman at his side? Poor Elmer, it must have burst his bubble.

She was not The Other Woman. Not really. He wouldn't have left me for her. I knew that. It was just an affair, "rising up out of the bottom of his life" to save him. I couldn't have saved him then, not with a screaming babe on my tit and a three-year-old blithering in the corner. I was no angel of mercy. Affairs happen. Now we were like all those other couples, learning to live with a breach of trust so wide you could drive a logging truck through it.

White Raven,

Indeed, Tom, in his mind, was still the innocent young man awkward with girls, a loser in high school. In his mind he was no cad, no deceitful womanizer.

And why did he need to confess this "innocent" affair? Did he really think this was the manly thing to do? The husbandly thing? The honest thing, now that I was strong enough to take it? That is not the smart way, not the European way. He did it to rid himself of the guilt. He wanted the slate clean. It was for himself. And now I had to find a way to live with it.

A month after Tom's confession, we were at Bernie's together, chickens and pigs wandering around, and while Bernie and Linda were making dinner in the front of the trailer, Tom and I climbed in the back, and I nearly had my way with him, I was so overwhelmed with lust. By some strange quirk of my female psyche, the thought of him with another woman brought out the tigress in me. I could not keep my hands off of him.

I had to accept the affair, but they had violated the red double-mummy love bed of the Montana mountains where we had hiked, the very sleeping bag where Benjamin was conceived! I dragged it down the steps into the crawl space below. He dragged it back up again, said he was sorry for what he did, but that the down bag was too good to waste.

That poor old sleeping bag was dragged up and down the steps all winter until one day it disappeared. Tom accused me of disposing of it. The truth is that I knew nothing. It was a true mystery. But if things do have spirits I can well imagine that the red down bag, tragic icon of love, pulled back and forth by the tug o'war between the man and woman, one day blew its seams—and fifty thousand goose down feathers exploded into the sky heading in the general direction of Canada whence they came, just as straight and fast as they could flutter.

I am staring at the CENTER POST
roped in place
soaring like a phallus into the wet gray sky
swaying gently with the winds
I want to smash your head against it
paint it red, my love,
and carve her name into the weathered wood

"Please," you say, "don't take this out on me
I am not that person now
What should I do—cry 'I'm sorry' on my knees,
make hot chocolate for you?"

No, not hot chocolate, my love
No apologies!
Get off your knees!
Defend yourself from this
inquisition, from your
shattered, sleepless lunatic of a wife

Protect yourself
As you have always done

CHAPTER 11

Balloon Love

"More belongs to marriage
than four legs in a bed"

- Rainer Rilke

I stayed. This was not the end of us. For here is my balloon theory of love: Everything is ruled by physical law. Why should love be different? When a balloon is blown up with air and let go, it races off zig-zagging and careening around until it is dissipated. When a huge balloon is blown up it, of course, takes longer to go through its wild gyrations, bumping into everything in its path, before finally fizzling out.

So, I reason, if love is born in a luscious state of heightened romance and great sex—if it is a huge Red Love Balloon—it will take much time and many aerial antics to dissipate it. Physical law.

I went on loving him, for he was not less than he was when we were at the zenith of our love. I couldn't stop loving him just because I hated him, just because I hurt, just because he seemed sometimes a total stranger.

When Tom and I conceived our love in the streets of San Francicso and set up house between the speakers in the Zone Called Paradise, even though we moved Romance to the mountains, stuffed it rudely into an eight-foot wide trailer, abused it with rain-warped living and a potpourri of flies, snakes, scorpions and spiders—our love, so burned into the psyche, into the cellular memory, into the divine place where the angels dwell—our love had staying power.

And so it zigged and zagged, dipped and rose, down, up, round and round, whirling, loop-de-looping around the hill that was our home, like some crazy drunken hawk that soared and circled there. Perhaps a love like this never really dies...it just eventually wears itself out, gets tired, seasick. And finally that last bit of air farts out of the flailing balloon leaving in its wake a shaky trail of sky-writing: the white-puffy words: The End

Love woman would stay until The End
was written in large puffy letters in the sky.

White Raven,
A balloon theory to explain my love? Yet it was true. I loved him, hated him, loved him. What can you do? It was a marriage of soul, and whenever there was a hole in the deep mire of our lives, love would push through like a purple thistle, and have its way.

CHAPTER 12

Goat Love

In addition to being a pothead, Tom was a milk-aholic. He could never get enough. In summer when he perspired, he reeked of sour milk; there was so much milk in him that it came out his pores. He drank so much milk that he had to have two goats impregnated just to feed his thirst. Jennifer came first, from folks up China Grade. She was bred with a buck at Camp Joy, a communal farm on the outskirts of Boulder Creek. When Jennifer came to us she was tethered out in the middle of the field to a post. Her instinctive need for shelter powered her loud cries in the middle of the night.

One morning she was missing. Tom searched the neighborhood for her, and finally found her down the road lying in a ditch, bleeding and weak. We called the mobile vet and he pronounced her stable but in shock. We learned that a pack of German Shepherd pups had broken loose and went in search of adventure. The vet said that once they had the taste of blood, they would be back. Tom could not sleep until Jennifer had a home.

I didn't know that a house could go up in a week. But it did. It was complete with two rooms, steps, roof, and windows. I almost made curtains for the fun of it, because—helas!— it was the only finished house (other than the house model) on the property. The bags of feed were stored in one of the rooms and a block of salt hung from a hook.

Jennifer was ornery. She only had eyes for Tom. Jealous of other females, she would try to charge me (and Sami once). One day she escaped her fence and began moving up the hill. Little Sami stood jumping up and down at the edge of the house screaming hysterically until Jennifer was herded back to her fenced-in yard down below.

Pregnant Snowflake arrived, an older goat with a cleft hoof curling up into the air. She was snowy-white, and unlike her housemate Jennifer, had a quiet disposition. They were due at about the same time, and, as is typical of hormonal females living in close quarters, they delivered on the same morning. We were there watching, Tom with his camera, Ben and Sami getting to hold the kids after they were licked clean.

Tom's life was defined by the milking of the goats. Once early in the morning. Once in the evening. It was his meditation. Between the morning and evening milking Tom would walk to town, a five-mile stroll down Big Basin Road, and then five miles back, smoking a joint along the way. He had a lot of thinking to do. His life had become walking, thinking, milking, and drinking (milk)—smoking goes without saying. The locals called him "the walking man." He drank a gallon of milk every day, partly because he loved it, partly because there would be another load the next day and the demand had to keep up with the supply.

> *All this milk! remarks The White Raven. Was this a reversion to childhood? A search for the Great Mother? Was he a* puer aeternus*—an eternal boy?*

I learned to milk the goats. Jennifer didn't charge me when I came alone; it was only when Tom was there that her jealousy was sparked. I was never comfortable around them, but how could I live on the land without being able to say, in future years, that I had milked the goats? However, I never learned to make goat cheese or goat butter or goat ice cream. I had my limits as a country wife.

A soft warm fog is wrapped around the earth tonight
easing slowly past the steady moon
Cricket song rings through the endless grey
a hundred voices all in unison
one tone so clear and clean
it is the same as silence

The goat bleats faintly down the hill
never sleeps
awaiting the ancient wolf

My husband sleeps
My children sleep
round white faces
floating in dreams
still as night flowers

PART 5

What The Princess of Peace Saw

"You don't get what you need
if you don't ask for it"

- Tom Corn

I sat watching you as you tapped seedlings
into the soil, your fingers
reverently patting down the dirt

I would not mind your fingers
on me, touching me in that way

Feed me   water me   talk to me
If you want to know what I need
ask the plants

CHAPTER 1

Cult in The Hills

IT WAS OUR FOURTH SUMMER in the Half-Built House. We decided that Tom would stay at home with Sami and Ben and be a househusband. I went out to find a job.

Maybe it was just the times, or maybe my propensity for weirdness, but when I took my job I stumbled from one bizarre situation at home, right into another one at work. Strange place. Strange people. Circle School was part of a cult called Christ Circle. The community and school were set on fifty acres of rolling hills, meadows and ponds, with dormitories and a large cafeteria where they ate their own produce and livestock. They were self-sufficient, except for the teachers (and me, the school secretary) who were hired from the outside.

As far as I could tell, the students whose parents couldn't handle them were probably just hyperactive or misfits in public school. They seemed okay to me. The school was a glorified military academy in the redwoods. The minute they entered, the children had to give up everything they owned: radios, books, money. They would horde pencils under their pillows just to have something. One young student named Joe took a fancy to one of the farm pigs. You could see him walking the pig on a leash on his time off, up and down the hills of the estate—a forlorn teenager walking a pig.

On Friday of my first week, Arthur Vogel, the leader of the cult, ushered me into his office, closed the door, instructed me to take notes for the letter he was about to send to his lawyer. I was to throw away the notes afterward and speak of this to no one. It was his suicide letter, and the date for his demise was to be that weekend. It was Friday and I had to do something. Before I left that day, I wrote Vogel a heart-felt letter about his beautiful school in the redwoods, and stuck it in his mail slot. At home, I tried in vain to reach the lawyer.

Monday he showed up for work. I was not too surprised, didn't really think he'd do it. His ego was much too big to snuff himself out. Maybe he was testing me for confidentiality. I began to wonder if I should quit and get a job bagging groceries at Erba's Market in town.

The women and men lived in separate quarters, even the married ones. Mother Sarah, an ex-hippie in her fifties, heard my story about the half-built house and decided right then that I belonged with them. Every few days she begged me to get out of my sorry situation and join their family. She gave me all her old hippie skirts (as if that were an incentive), and taught me to use the IBM composer, precursor to the computer—my first introduction to a machine that could remember and think. That was a good thing.

At a school assembly, Arthur Vogel explained their world to them: "We of Christ Circle are from Orion. There is a shield around this land that will protect us. We have information that the world will come to an end on the 26th of March, next year. We are safe here. We need nothing from the world."

CHAPTER 2

Your Little Red-Haired Girl

Her eyes are wide and inviting as the sunrise
Her voice is smooth as dark sand
Her face is open as a child's face and—
behind it is a woman saying "yes"
and then again, "yes."

THAT SUMMER WHILE I WORKED, Tom took Ben and Sami every day to Forest Pool down Big Basin Road. It was the old community pool with a faded Coca Cola sign from the 50s and a hot dog stand. Sami and Ben learned to swim and got so sunburned day after day, they never stopped peeling.

Fall came and, with it, school. Sami, now four, was signed up for pre-school at the Good Shepherd Church. I was at the Village Laundry the Sunday before school started, and I had a conversation with Lenore, a woman in long skirts with soft brown curls and large doe eyes who sang and played guitar for children. She told me she was a co-teacher at the Good Shepherd pre-school, and as I folded laundry a scene was planted in my mind that grew wild as thistles. It stayed with me like a vision all that evening. It was in my head when I awoke the next morning and I took it, wrenched in my gut, to work: Tom delivers Sami to the school; he is struck dumb by the beauty and charm of Lenore, and life changes in that moment— forever after.

Call it fate. Call it seeing the future. Or call it knowing your husband and recognizing what you already know will be irresistible to him—a woman who devours him with her eyes, makes him feel good, special, worthy. I had seen this vision with such clarity, felt it with such a chilling charge of terror that I returned home panicky, dreading what I already knew.

Other Woman had finally come.

When I arrived home from work the first thing I saw was a note on the table. It said: "For safety's sake, be sure that Sami wears shoes tomorrow."

"You sent her to school without shoes on?"

"I could only find one, so I figured barefoot was better than being late."

"God, she's not an urchin. How embarrassing."

Then, it began. He told me about Lenore. He could not stop. I listened in a haze. Past present and future were all confused. Powerful instinct told me that this was the beginning of the unraveling of our marriage, the demise of the half-built house on the hill, the undoing of this whole crazy saga. In that moment, listening and watching, I could not stop the sense of doom that was sinking into every single molecule of my world.

You are Charlie Brown
and she is your little red-haired girl
she makes you blush

He was obsessed, and in the coming weeks my househusband began to invite his new playmate over while I was at work. She walked around the half-built house, amazed at the massive beams, the rounded deck of the living room without walls. Seeing all this for the first time, she brought light into the bleakness of this squalor and made the dream seem fresh and real again for him. She knew how to please a man, how to cast a spell and pull him slowly in.

Sometimes they would go to her house, a rented cabin in a sunny clearing on Moonbeam Lane. Sami and Ben would play outside and Lenore and Tom would hang out on the deck. I knew all this because he told me everything. So much did he want me to know that this was all right, that he carefully explained how they touched but were not sexual—how they loved, but were not lovers.

"But you're in love with her. I can feel it. Can you tell me that you're not?"

"Well sure I am, but you can be in love with more than one person. This is new. The intensity will pass. I promise you. I'm not going anywhere. I can't help what's happening. Don't make it more than it is."

But neither could I make it less. I could think of nothing else. At work. At home. In the car. I saw her face, her big brown eyes. She was in our home, in my dreams—strange recurring dreams. She would float in quietly between me and Tom on the bed without a word. Just a silent presence. A sorceress. Dressed in black. Wearing a ring on her finger. Offering herself to him.

She had a way with men. She was a fountain of pheromones—the perfect archetype of seductress—her power from some deep, timeless, primordial place.

White Raven,
You might well ask why Lenore is not depicted more as a person, for surely she had a heart and pain and her own story. She played guitar and sang to children. She was honored in the community.

After all, I was once a seductress too, parading my sexy self around, spraying pheromones out in all directions. But for me she was so long a dreaded presence, so long a haunting phantom, that I could not then give her human attributes, but rather those of a nixie, a siren with the gift of song. I felt her attraction the way he felt it. The three of us were connected in a mystical triangle in dreams and in life that held us with so strong a force there was no way out, except to live it. I was as helpless as a wriggling bug in a spider web.

We were both consumed with her—a perfect folie a deux.

CHAPTER 3

Swastika

VOGEL WAS A MAN WITH a spell so pervasive it spread like a shadow over the fifty green acres, and the shield around Christ Circle was not from Orion; it was his own charisma, holding, protecting the flock.

Things continued to get weirder. The local press reported that the leaders had been embezzling Federal funds through loan packages to a network of beauty colleges they had set up in the Bay Area. They had me typing balance sheets on a daily basis and each day the figures were revised. Vogel's suicide letter was beginning to make sense. He was in deep trouble. His world was crumbling.

Passports were ordered for all the family members and some of the students, as well. Vogel announced their imminent departure for Germany. Vogel, it turns out, was of Jewish origin, his own parents having died in a concentration camp. The return to Germany was some kind of perverse fixation with Nazism.

The teachers of Circle School who lived on the outside were uneasy. One day they came to school and found the Swastika flag hung on the high wall of the dining hall. They all quit.

News helicopters were flying around the school to see what they could see. Vogel addressed the school (and the listening press) proclaiming: "The swastika is an ancient symbol of the wheel of life. I put it up to teach you that a symbol can't hurt you." With helicopters flying around and the Feds on his back, it was hardly the time to put up swastikas for a lesson on symbolism. This man liked to be in the spotlight, he liked to bait the establishment, and he liked drama.

My duties as secretary came to an abrupt end. It was teachers they needed. I was recruited to teach French in the mornings and English in the afternoon. I wanted to see how this would end, but most of all, I wanted my unemployment insurance. Two weeks later I was called into the office and was told that my services were no longer required. They were all leaving. Mother Sarah made one last plea for me to come along.

They didn't go to Germany. The last I heard they ended up in Booneville, California, and according to the news, they absconded with some of the children whose parents charged them with kidnapping. I never got my unemployment insurance because they had not paid anything into the system. It was as if none of this had ever happened. I returned home, without a job.

You were used to an evening mommy
a read me a story, tuck me in bed mommy
Now, here am I looming before you
at the sink, the counter, everywhere
and you are filled with
gargantuesque need

Forgive me   but
I long to be silent,
invisible doing dishes
just another person in the room

Love, Mommy (someday you will understand)

CHAPTER 4

Love in The Cracks

If this thing with Lenore was leading the way to the demise of our marriage, there was no thunderclap, no fanfare announcing the end; rather a pervasive cloud of doom. They didn't sleep together. They were only co-conspirators in a spiritual affair that was not meant to play itself out on this earthly plane. He had mythicized this union, anointed it with the juice of his imagination, and I was sure it stoked his fantasies more than it did hers. I do not think she lived for his attentions. Why couldn't she find some other married man to love, to unsettle? Why him? Why now?

"You can love two women," he said without guilt. As for me? That he loved her did not make me love him less. It made me want him more. I looked at him—his curly head, his long lanky body, and I went on wanting him, in this new unholy poly-amorous alliance. After all, hadn't I already been living with the phantom Other Woman all our married life? I wanted him, and yet I felt deep down that this was the kiss of death.

He tried. He gave me tenderness and physical love which was always the measure of our marriage. He never meant for this to be the end of us.

He made paper airplanes with Ben and sailed them off the deck. He played with the children. A man in love has love to give. He pulled out the old hand-cranked ice cream maker from the San Francisco days, bought rock salt, cream, eggs, and vanilla, and sat on the steps churning it as the kids watched in wonder. They didn't know you could make ice cream.

I learned to live with Other Woman just as I had learned to live with the Justine affair, with the flies, just as I had learned that a half-built house could be a home. I didn't look for endings. I clung to comfort in the little things; I lived for love in the cracks.

One evening I walked into the dark hallway, and my eyes were shocked by a one hundred-watt bulb shining naked on Ben's globe. Tom and Ben were kneeling on the floor, the globe between them. They were turning it slowly round, and the light was casting half the world into darkness. The father voice was explaining how the northern hemisphere was always in sunlight, and the boy could see that it was so.

a man and a boy bent over a globe
they are an illustration in a science book
it is a beginning
it is something

CHAPTER 5

The Comfort Zone

Marijuana, dope, ganja, weed, doobie, joint, roach, rolling paper, pipe, felony, misdemeanor, seeing God, the cosmos, narc, narcotic, illegal, underground, herb, high, music, sex, orgasm, breathing, breathing, paranoia, police, guard dog, guns, green consciousness, photosynthesis, reefer madness, dope, dopey, money, 150 an ounce, 2000 a pound, folk grower, plantation grower, sensimilla, helicopters, flowers, cannabis, ultra weed, Indica, Setiva, Thai weed, Buddha Bud, Maui Wowie, heavy high, "Hey Man, this is the kind, smell it, yeah good taste, primo, primo. This is the kind."

I am sitting here in a hidden garden behind my house watching nature do what she has been doing for millions of years—photosynthesis—sunlight pouring onto green exotic leaves. The leaves are spread like ribs of a fan, turning up to catch the rays. Tall, green, spindly plants delicately pruned, the leaves no longer producing new growth, their energy turning now to the flowers that are growing frostier with the cool breath of each new day; buds with lavender and white frost glowing like halos in the sun.

It is nearly harvest time in the mountains. My genius husband who can do anything, has turned his genius to the growing of these precious weeds. Three years ago a friend gave him one plant. He called it Christmas Tree because it was shaped like one. He groomed it, guarded it, worried over it all summer and harvested it in the fall. One plant. Christmas Tree. That's how it all began.

I am sitting in the middle of a nursery of hanging plants, thirty different varieties of sensimilla and various cross breeds. The parents of these plants live in faraway lands: Hawaii, Cambodia, Thailand, Africa, Afghanistan, Nepal. An international community thrives here behind this house, hidden by the metal corrugated blind. They seem happy enough in California. Even plants have had a natural migration to the western shore. Why wouldn't they be happy weeds? They are fed, watered, caressed and loved.

An airplane cruises overhead and Tom jumps out on the deck to watch it circle once over our house. Ben follows, asking, "Why do the police put people in jail for having marijuana?"

"Well," says Tom, rolling a joint, "someday they won't. The laws are not always right, but they are still laws."

The airplanes and helicopters are thick as flies this time of year. Up River Road some friends of ours got busted. The cops ravaged the land, sliced up mattresses, broke some Buddha statues. It is in their job description. It is their job to destroy the plants, throw things around, and take the weed away, but people seldom go to jail. Folk growers, we call ourselves. Only those with plantations get put away. They are too greedy.

The real threat is the punks who rip off the growers, punks with guns. The rules of capitalism apply in bootlegging as in the real world. Supply and demand, middlemen, competition. The difference is that in bootlegging there is no protection from the law and paranoia abounds. Fear of strangers. Distrust of visitors. Rules for the children who grow up slightly underground. The weed that's supposed to make you high, mellow you out, becomes the cause of fear, theft, bad vibes, guns and violence.

We live in a deserted construction zone in the warp of time. We are folk growers, just trying to make some money to get our house done, just trying, as always, to get to the Comfort Zone.

Lately I have begun Talking to God – 1981

It is seven years now that we are on this hill
Seven years. . . and I, moving ever closer to my senses
to my hungry need for a tranquil scene to create
what I have to create
Seven years in this wasteland. I ask you God,
Is this the Cosmic Joke?
Tell me if it is time to laugh

But there is a certain poetry worming along
in all this rubble
Maybe I am the poetry
And what keeps me here year after year, God,
is the same thing that keeps the flies
It is our home

I talk of renting a place this winter
a little cabin with small-paned windows, braided rug
and walls—something with walls and a roof
But it is hard to imagine calling it home
It would probably be small and dark
and its possibilities would be only finite

On this hill, God, the possibilities are forever and ever
Everything is in the budding stage
year after year after year
Seven years
a millionth of a second of eternity
a slap on the bottom of a newborn babe
a sneeze, a pinprick of time

We are in an epoch on this hill
and I have learned
that on this odyssey there is only temporary
and if you try to step out of your story
you will only stumble into another one

We sleep outside now on our platform
under the pines
I am grateful for the way the wind
brushed through the trees this morning as we loved
and for the bird calls coming together around us
like a bouquet of wildflowers

There will be summer days like this

CHAPTER 6

The Greener Creatures

TRINA LIVED IN A LOG house hidden on the other side of the pine trees behind us. While out taking a walk on her land one day she happened by our sleeping platform in the trees behind the house, and heard us in the act of doing what we did best. This piqued her curiosity so she came over one evening to meet the platform people. She was an attractive blond with flashing white teeth and sky blue eyes. She spoke in a silvery voice. She was earnest, direct, self-sufficient, a woman to be reckoned with. She was no threat to me—not Tom's cup of tea.

Once she found out what we were up to, she invited us over to see her greenhouse full of maturing exotic plants. She and Tom had plenty to talk about—shop talk. She and I had much to talk about too. She was a writer, into her second book. She was writing about a woman named California (Cal) who went west and discovered the "greener creatures," a psycho-physical melding of marijuana and humans.

Trina lived like a hermit up there in her log house, writing and growing. She rolled cigarettes. She had an espresso machine. A typewriter. It was nearing harvest, and she was homebound day and night. Her house became a refuge for me. Woman talk. Good coffee.

Tom smoked weed all the time. That was the beauty of growing, and not only did it provide quantity, but quality and choice. There were jars lined up that had names or symbols. One plant was good for listening to music. One was great for sex (brand X). One, for thinking, one for working, one for parties—an endless potpourri of smoke. There was even one I kept for my own. It was mild and never caused paranoia. I never touched the others (except for brand X).

I never knew Tom Corn not stoned. In his San Francisco Lockheed days the moment he got home he lit up, and weekends were a stony, love-making marathon. But in the trailer days he couldn't always afford to buy a lid. One time when he ran out, he was a mad dog tearing around, ransacking the trailer for dried-up roaches to scrape together into something smokable. I stayed out of his way. And when Jack and Jennifer, the Born Again Christians next door, announced they were giving up all their old habits and had buried their pot in the yard, Tom was seen down on his knees digging through the dirt.

The growing became everything. Project man was on. These were living things, dependent on him, and if they were treated royally, they would give back tenfold what he was giving to them; they were growing money for our house. Tom became a sorcerer of plants, nurturing and protecting and fussing over every sticky leaf.

But the house remained in limbo. It was stoned too, like its master. The status quo was sunk into the weathering floorboards of the living room deck, the torn mylar windows, the moldy old rugs.

The next stage was to have been the welding of the brackets that were to hold the spoke wheel beams to the center post. For reasons I didn't understand, the welding project was on permanent hold. Growing pot became the project of choice.

CHAPTER 7

The Good Father

THUNDER DELI, SANTA CRUZ

My father came west on business, then stayed for two days to be with us. I left him at the gas pump in town where he was driving on to San Francisco to catch a flight to Detroit, then go on in his Mercedes to Toledo—home to my beautiful mother, back to his retirement and his easy chair by the fireplace, his oil painting and his sculpture and his meditation and his ever-expanding life. I want to call him back and tell him how I love him, in case there is any doubt, but by now he is up in the plane in the friendly skies of United. Oh Daddy, please drive carefully when you get to Detroit. It will be dark and maybe raining, and you can't see well at night.

My children adore him. He is their "grandpaw," and he makes them feel special. We took him to Roaring Camp this morning. I wanted him to see that for my children there is a duck pond too, like the one at Oak Openings where he would take us. We went for a walk on the loop trail, winding through great burly redwoods. Sorrel spread like a lush carpet in the open spaces. The world was singing with color.

He put Sami on his shoulders and bounced her piggyback down the trail. She laughed and laughed. His hair was bluish in the light of after-rain. I got a flash of childhood, a whiff of pure joy mixed with pure sadness. . .And I am a little girl again, walking with my Daddy on a Sunday morning in Ottawa Park, my hand in his warm hand, past the split trunk tree where the dwarves lived. Daddy, how did your hair get so white? And will my children remember? And how will I make sure that they remember?

On our return, we all stood in the living room of our half-built house with plastic and rug walls. "It's cozy here," he said. Yes, I thought. It isn't so cozy here, but what he is feeling is that we are a family. For Tom that is not easy, not natural. But I no longer wait for him to be what my father is. He is what he is and he will be what he will be, and we are a family in our own way.

Standing in our living room, my father looked out the mylar window at the metal-sided shed and asked, "What's that for?" I was in the back room and I heard Tom say, "I grow plants in there." And then I thought I heard him say, "I grow marijuana plants." He might have said it was a tool shed, but he didn't. He said to my father, "I plant marijuana in there," and then I stood at the threshold of the living room to listen. Tom said, "Well, actually, I've been wanting to talk to you about this for a long time. That's how we hope to finish our house. I have a good crop this year."

And my father in his ever-even tone asked question after question, never having met anyone who grew marijuana, and here was his son-in-law, not to mention his daughter, in the bootlegging pot business of the '80s. His only contact with marijuana was his younger cousin and business associate who is avant-garde (in Toledo!), did primal therapy, encounter groups, and marijuana.

My father is a prudent man, a liberal man who lived through the Depression, a businessman who makes the right decisions over and over. His extra money is in Swiss banks and Mexican gold. Yet he took a chance and lent us forty thousand dollars to buy our land and to build our house. The money has flowered into a yard full of broken toilets and piles of used wood, coils of copper tubing, a driveway gone back to nature, the gravel lost in forests of lush thistle bushes, and at the top of the hill there sits this half-built gigantic house of redwood timbers milled by locals, a house three times the size my father built for a family of eight.

Tom, with his usual tact, informed my father that people over fifty don't really have any idea about what's going on, that they are living in the past. My father who is sixty-eight didn't flinch a bit. My father does not live in a vacuum. He simply asked questions, listening with serious attention about how the plants are grown, how big they get, what they are worth, what the risks are. There was a simple desire to know, to understand, to comprehend how this could be a business, how this could be a solution to a problem. He asked questions and

Tom answered them, as though they had been discussing the weather system in the Santa Cruz mountains, and I thought, This can't be happening, but it was. . . and Tom had done what I couldn't do, because I was still my father's little girl, wanting to do the right thing, wanting to protect.

That morning walking through the woods, my father had told me he had respect for alternative lifestyles, but he was worried simply that Tom had lost his enthusiasm for building the house, that it had turned into an unhealthy burden. And who can deny that it is a burden? Who can deny Tom's body sweats at 2:00 in the morning? Who can deny the soaking wet sheets? People who look up at our house on the hill might think that we moved into an old abandoned ruin. It is known at the County Building Department as the Carpet House. We just go on with our lives, as if a house with plastic walls were another twentieth century mode of habitat, as if it had some validity.

As I write this, I am sitting in the Thunder Deli drinking coffee and eating a huge piece of chocolate cake. It helps me to write, the cake. It is rich and comforting and smells of home and childhood. It is like the chocolate cake that Mom used to bake before she found out, after we all grew up, that it is bad for you, and started making from-scratch bran muffins with honey and raisins. But it didn't hurt us, the cake. We thrived on it, all six of us. We grew tall and healthy on it and went out into the world to choose what we chose.

For me it was not the nice Jewish man under suburban skies. And yet there was the night when I was watching Fiddler on the Roof *for the third time, crying silently into my popcorn, wondering. . . and if there had been a nice Jewish man? And if. . .*

You see, when your childhood is easy, when love comes as easily as milk from the breast, when getting what you need comes as easily as to a tree in an open meadow catching sunshine on its leaves, you grow up thinking this marriage will be easy. What I had never considered was that those of us who find it so easy are the chosen few, and we don't often find each other to marry, but seek out those who are the stifled trees trying to grow on a craggy hillside with rocks for soil in a thick grove that blocks its sun. There are those trees too, and the marriage is not easy, and the love does not flow like sap, and the leaves fall one by one to the ground.

Why does it hurt so, to think of Childhood? Why does it hurt so when I smell a brush fire in California that reminds me of autumn leaves burning on Drummond Road? Why is it so painful to see this father growing old and white, this mother with her moonface, once so large, soft powdered skin across high Russian cheekbones. The last time I saw her, her moonface was small, and the skin hung loosely, as if her face had shrunk. Mommy, Daddy, Daddy, Mom: you gave me everything, everything. . . except my future. That is where I stepped in. That is where everything changed. But it was a lovely past, and thank you.

CHAPTER 8

Harvest Time

Some mornings I would wake up surprised
to find myself lying flat on my back, barely breathing
legs straight out, feet together
hands crossed on my chest

This is the death position, I would shudder
and will I really die young
as I have always felt?

IT WAS A MONTH FROM harvest time. Tom had to stay at home protecting his crop, but we decided to risk a short trip to Deejins Big Sur Inn, our getaway place. We even consulted our Gemini handbook which promised that these were romantic days for us. It was the right thing to do.

Tom rigged up lights that would go on at dark, watered the plants, and the day before our departure he phoned Lenore and invited her over to give Ben a guitar lesson.

"Why today, just before we go away together?" I asked. "We plan one romantic outing this whole year and I have to leave with her face in the front of my mind? It's like we're taking her with us." And later after she left, I couldn't stop. "So tell me this, honestly: Have you ever thought about the possibility of living with her?"

"Yes, I thought about it that time you talked about the feeling you've always had that you would die young. If that really happened, it would be probable I'd get together with her at some point, but as long as we are together, I'll never leave you. I promise you that."

" You give me fidelity because I happen to be alive?"

"I love you and I do want to be with you, and I want you to live, but how can you ever make promises about the future? I'm doing the best I can."

CHAPTER 9

The Angry Father

The Big Sur Inn no longer takes reservations
so we drive two hours
not knowing if there is a room
Do you like to walk? asks the woman at the desk
There is one room in the Top House

The ocean is framed in the window
blue fog steaming off the hills
A petite grey cat is curled on the bed
looking us over
as Tom rolls a joint
Cat of the Top House
how many lovers have you seen
pass through this room
here and gone, here and gone
while the ocean stays framed in the window

Rounded rocks peek out of the ocean waters
dark green manes of seaweed
tossing their hair with each passing wave
haughtily, like ancient harlots

The skin of the sea stretches and gives
rippling to the shore
The shore rock suns itself
waiting for the next wave
The ocean comes
and the shore rock, warm,
accepting as a fat lover, shudders,
white foam rolling up her smooth,
round surface
There is more passion in the sea

THE NEXT MORNING TOM SET the timer for the house lights, we dropped Sami and Ben at Omland, and left for Big Sur.

When we returned home, Tom checked the metal shed behind the house. The plants were gone, savagely torn and severed at the base, remnants scattered all over the ground. The plants were ripped off before they were even mature. Our house was raped, its salvation doomed.

He stood, an interminable quiet before the storm, at the edge of the living room without walls, staring into the mountains. Then his eyes landed down the hill on the house across Big Basin Way where some new people had just moved in. His quiet desperation ballooned into a blood-red rage, as he grabbed a two-by-four and stormed down the hill, crossed the street, and I watched dumbfounded as he smashed the windows of their VW bug. He kept on swinging until every window was in pieces.

I was afraid, very afraid.

The men across the street, it turns out, were Christians, good people. They did not make a fuss. Maybe they saw that Tom was someone to steer clear of. They only asked that he give them money to replace the windows.

After the rip-off, Tom had the look of a desperate man. He would have to come up with some other scheme to produce money to finish the house. His radar was on. He discovered a black walnut orchard up in Stanislaus County that was felling all the mature trees that were no longer producing. He contacted the owner and we drove up there and took a walk through the orchard, Tom seeing dollar signs in the thick trunks of black walnut.

His plan was to collect the felled trees, load them into a truck, drive them home and slice them into magnificent pieces that could be sold to wood dealers and furniture makers. But where would the money come from to make this all happen?

My father, where else? Now that he and my dad had talked candidly about his marijuana enterprise, he felt that he had achieved a rapport with this enlightened businessman. He begged me to call my father for a loan. I refused, knowing that was a very bad idea; he had already said that he couldn't lend any more. But he bullied me into calling. I made the call trembling, and delivered this outrageous proposition. He listened, and in a tone I had never heard in my entire life, I heard my father outraged, gruff, and insulted. He said he could not lend another dime to this project, that he had five other children to consider, that he was concerned about our ability to pay back what we had already borrowed. He hung up abruptly.

I had never known my father's anger. I knew that he would find the way to forgive me, but his lack of faith in us gave weight to my already flagging sense of hope and entitlement.

CHAPTER 10

The Princess of Peace

going to Grandma's
moving down the track,
clickety-clack, clickety-clack
watching the lavender mountains
and the brown and white cows
scattered like Fisher-Price toys
in these storybook hills
I want to run up a velvet green hill
in a flowing white gown
reach up and embrace the
turquoise sky
like a Greek nymph in a
Maxfield Parrish painting

It was Christmas and we were riding the train to L.A. to stay with Grandma and Grandpa. Somehow being with your in-laws at Christmas always makes a shaky marriage seem a valid, substantial thing. Tom's mother and I were close, always had been. We drank Martinis and had a good laugh in the evenings. We shopped together, cooked, played duets on the piano.

Tom called an old high school buddy, someone he played Little League with when he was young. His friend Jerry was now member of a spiritual community called Morningland. He invited us to a ceremony the next evening.

Men and women stood outside the building smoking cigarettes, waiting for the doors to open. We were led into the main lobby where publications were handed out and books sold. Everywhere hung pictures of the spiritual leader: "The Princess of Peace"—born in New York, a psychic and a seer.

We sat in a church-like assembly hall. New Age Music accompanied the procession of the Princess to the stage. She was a middle-aged woman with long blond hair, a flowing white gown and a crown of flowers in her hair.

People were invited to come to her, one at a time, for a psychic reading. As people approached the throne she gave a channeling and a single rose. When it was my turn, I stood up and she said, "But wait—you are not alone, and pointing to Tom: "That is your husband, is he not? And you are double Gemini. Come up together," she said, smiling. The audience laughed.

We approached her chair, and as I came into her aura I felt a warm energy surrounding us; I could not stop smiling. It was a feeling of lightness and well-being. She spoke to me:

"For the past two years you have been going through the most insecure period of your life. This will change in the new year. There will be a shift. I am seeing your child self now. She is sweet and whole and angelic. She feels special. Is that not so?"

"Yes. I was loved as a child."

I walked out holding my yellow rose with a warmth and optimism I hadn't felt in months. She saw me as a child. She saw My Laurie Me.

Just as Tom had promised, the intensity of Lenore did not last. She decided to marry the cook in the Apple Cafe where she worked as waitress. It didn't seem a likely match—but we were all there to witness it in the garden of her house on Moonbeam Lane. The November day was sunny, full of light and color. There were flowers in her hair. Children played in the yard. Tables full of dishes brought by all the guests. Bleating of the goats at the far end of the yard.

Tom feigned a fatherly, approving attitude about the marriage. I think he was in great pain, but I think he also understood that he and Lenore were not a match on this earthly plane. Theirs was a soul connection.

In the crowd was a tall willowy woman with long chestnut hair and a smile flashing white teeth. She was alone. Her name was Katrina. Her voice was sultry and bedroom, and she had a low, soft laugh. She moved slowly through the crowd, every motion studied and graceful as a model. She and Tom stood talking while I went off with the children to play in the green grass.

CHAPTER 11

Mile-Long Walk

There is a dinner guest at my house
I am on my way home
There are butterflies no, there are
bats in my stomach

Tom: Oh, you'll like her
You may even know her from somewhere
Yes, I will surely know her, because
she will remind me of me, a little
These women are my complements
the parts of me I do not have

I must look my best
I must enter the room with a swirl and a flair
but what if they are on the deck
sitting on the couch that looks out
on the redwood mountains
what then?
what of my entrance?

IT SEEMS THAT LENORE'S MARRIAGE had created an Other Woman vacuum. Tom announced one night that a woman he had met in town would be our guest for dinner. "You don't have to worry," he said. "You'll like her. She knows I am a married man and monogamous. And don't worry about dinner. I'm taking care of that."

I returned home from my writing group and found them on the deck talking. As I walked in she turned to look at me, and I knew at once that she did not really expect to see me there. Her dress was a giveaway. It was a long, blue, flowing dress with a plunging neckline revealing ample breasts. She was tall with long brown curls and a kind, open face. Did she think his fictitious wife was just a ploy to get her over? Or then again, maybe she did believe there was a wife and came prepared for a threesome.

In any case, Tom busied himself in the kitchen making pasta, and she and I sat on the deck drinking wine, having a good time. I was feeling the upper hand here, being the real wife and all. She was a bit sheepish with her breasts begging for attention, and kept pulling her dress up. We both got buzzed and silly.

She never came again, but that was not the end of dinner guests.

One afternoon, after shopping, I found the children home alone. "Where's Daddy?"

"He's taking a walk with his friend." After some probing I learned that His friend was Katrina, the sultry woman at Lenore's wedding. "She was over here lots of days this week," reported Sami. I knew that sooner or later Tom would seek her company, but why the secrecy?

They came walking up the steps. She entered as if she belonged there, said hello to me with her glistening white-tooth smile. I was flustered, freaking out, trying to cover it up. Tom spent the evening being very protective of her, as if to shelter her from his possibly hostile wife. He paid attention to me too, but in a tentative sort of way. I drank too much wine.

Conversation about our beautiful future house. The view. Tom walking her down the hill to her car. The sound of the motor. Tom walking back up the steps. He, doing what I knew he would do. He held me close and said he loved me. We went to bed. I waited for an explanation, but as always, he fell asleep like a baby.

My mind raced. *What am I doing wrong that I drive this man to hang out with other women? Maybe he just needs friends, and women would always be better company. Who could argue with that?* I grabbed my pillow, wrote an accusative letter about everything from the lack of heat in the house to the games with women, and this wasn't the sort of marriage I wanted. I dumped.

Headachy from the wine, I slept until noon. He was sitting at the redwood round table morose, the note in front of him. We spent the day moping around each other. By evening I knew I had to get out to walk. The one-mile walk down Big Basin to the Country Club had become my thinking place. I walked it often.

As I was starting down the stairs, I noticed Ben's muddy boots on the living room rug. "Ben," I shouted, "don't drag your muddy boots into the house. Leave them by the stairs." Startled, he looked at me, picked up his boots. I turned and fled down the stairs.

It was about 5:30, just before sundown. As I came to the fork of China Grade and Big Basin, a friend of ours, Dan, drove by with a car full of kids. He said, "I'm dropping the kids off at home, then going back to town. How about having a drink with me?" When had this ever happened?

"Sure," I said, thinking that it would be good to hang out with him, get some town life, get some attention, get out of this funk. "Sure," I said.

"I won't be long," said Dan. "Watch for me."

So I continued my mile-long walk toward the Country Club. When I got to the place where I usually turned around, Dan still hadn't shown up. It was getting dark but I kept on walking. There was a voice telling me it was time to get back home. . . *getting dark, getting late,* but I kept on walking, on past the Country Club toward the far end of the golf course. When I was almost to the bridge, I was surprised by quick running steps behind me. I was grabbed from behind and pulled into the bushes.

"Do you see this," he snarled, pointing to the gun in his hand. "Don't scream or I'll blow your fuckin' head off." He demanded to know my name.

"Nancy," I stammered. He seemed crazed, and kept asking how to get to Berkeley. He held the gun to my head the whole time.

"You're going to take me home with you. Where do you live?"

"I have children. I can't take you home."

"How many children do you have?"

And then from the deepest part of me came a voice that I did not recognize. "Three. Three children. I am a mother of three. Don't do anything to hurt me. I have children to take care of."

He pulled me into the brush and with the gun in my back ordered me to take off my clothes. I lay naked in the cold. He raped me there in the bushes of the golf course. I could hear cars passing by on Big Basin. I had flashes of my last words to Ben—yelling at him about his muddy boots.

I was saved by my own blood. I was bleeding hard. He backed off. "You didn't tell me you were on the rag, bitch!" He told me to count to twenty, then run. I threw on my jeans and sweatshirt, terrified that he would shoot me in the back and I would be found in the creek. I ran to the first condo and knocked on the door. Frantic woman, disheveled, blue jeans on inside out. They said they didn't have a phone and closed the door in my face.

I ran to the Club House phone booth, had no money for a call. A car pulled up with a young man in it. I told him I was attacked. He gave me a dime and I called Tom. In minutes the police were there to take me away. Tom stayed with the children.

Dominican Hospital. Lab tests. Tubes of blood to test for VD, alcohol. I was in shock and they could not draw blood. Veins retracted. A hematoma bulging from my arm. Pull out twenty pubic hairs. Pull out twenty hairs from my head. Stray hairs that are not mine are evidence. The hospital wall was lined with little boxes labeled Sexual Abuse Kit. I was bleeding all over everything. They took my clothes, put them in a bag. I had no clothes.

I called Tom. He was at first unwilling to come with clothes for me—said he was so tired, but finally he arrived, reluctant and morose—the children dragging in his wake.

The next day we went to the sheriff's office. I made a composite face from the brief glance I had in the dark. I answered questions. Questions, over and over.

The Santa Cruz Sentinel carried the story of a second rape on Irwin Way in Boulder Creek. The Country Club was no longer a safe place to walk. In my life, I was raped again by a complete stranger, and wondering why.

CHAPTER 12

Quicksand

He: *"All I ever wanted was for you to be strong and independent."*
Me: *"Then why do you tell me how to stir my tea?"*

FOR TWO WEEKS I WAS held together by rubber bands. Tamar took Sami, Ben and me to the place by the road past the Country Club where it had happened. They walked in a circle around the spot, Tamar burning sage and chanting, to purify the ground. I went about my days.

Then, one day the rubber bands snapped. I could not stop crying. While sitting reading Dr. Seuss to Sami, I broke into tears. Watching a sunset from the deck I broke. While making dinner, when the goats called, when Ben walked up the hill after school, I cried. I came undone.

And then, finally, in bed, I asked Tom, "Why did this happen? What is Katrina to you? Why haven't we talked about this? Why weren't you there for me? I was raped!"

"Well, I've been wanting to talk about it, but I was too weak because you didn't seem very receptive to it, and I couldn't stand another put-down. I brought her over here because I thought we had an understanding that we can bring our friends over to our house."

"Our friends, our friends? And how am I supposed to act when your friends who all happen to be women are here in my face? Tell me, how am I supposed to act?"

"That's what I mean. You don't have to act any way. You can get to know her too. Maybe you'll like her. She came with the clear understanding that I am a monogamous man. I told her that I felt drawn to her at the wedding and that I'm not looking for an affair. She liked that. She came over the next day and three other times. I couldn't tell you. I knew it would be trouble. I just wish you were not so emotionally dependent."

A week later while I was in town, a truck pulled up. David got out—my Neuropsychic healer, the one who had introduced me to my spirit baby after the abortion. He was my own personal genie on call, rising out of a bottle —or a truck.

"I heard about what happened and read about it in the paper. How are you doing?"

"I'm doing Okay, but you know—marriage problems."

"Is that what the rape was all about?"

"I guess you could say that. I wouldn't have been taking a walk so late in the evening otherwise. It was weird. I know I heard a voice telling me to go home. But I didn't listen, and then the boogie man jumped me."

" Sit down. I want to tell you something."

We sat at the bench in front of Erba's Market and David said, "Listen, if your house were burning down what would you grab first?"

"My kids."

"And after that?"

I hesitated.

"Look, kid, you'd better get this straight. Your kids come first. You have that right. Second is yourself. Third is your husband and your crazy marriage, and fourth is the crazy house. Okay? You were out walking and nearly got killed because of the marriage and the house. You've got it backwards. If I were you I would take the kids and rent a place somewhere for awhile. Don't make them suffer for your marriage."

It was January. A time of change, said the Princess of Peace. She was right after all. A near-death experience will do that for you. You clean your house, clear out the cobwebs. The house seemed more sad than tragic. Tom seemed more the fool on the hill than a fallen hero.

Tom and Ben and Sami are in L.A.
Nothing remains of them
but a teddy bear left on the couch
Here, today, when the house is not busy with
the noise of life
I can listen to my dream
to my voice screaming
my fists tight
my face wretched
Here in this silence
I hear the voice within me chanting
go
go now
or you will never

Again and again, the question: Why did I stay? Why did I not join the trail of feminists walking away from ruinous lives? So many times my hand was on the door, and yet I stayed.

We humans are fools in time, says The White Raven. Looking back we see it all so clearly, wondering how we could have stayed so long, our feet in the quicksand. Aha, but that is it! Rewinding is easy. Fast-forwarding is another matter. When you are standing in quicksand you do not know whether you'll get out. You do not say: "In twenty years I will be looking back on this; it will be but a story." When you are in quicksand you are stuck, and slowly sinking.

And no one else can tell you to when it is time to go, any more than they can tell a baby when it is time to birth itself, or an old withered woman on a daybed, when it is time for her to go. No one else was there to see the moments of tenderness, to look with sadness at his torn up hands and his shoes held together with duct tape—no one else to feel the lust, the alchemical bond that held us.

My poetry kept me; it was a ballast, a balm for pain so gripping, so intense, it was almost divine.

CHAPTER 13

By The Madrone Tree

Today I took the path up quail Hollow Ranch, stopped at the first look-out bench to write a few lines. These days I carry a pen and paper in a fanny pack wherever I go. Before, if I got a line and thought I'd remember it later, I grieved for it when I didn't. It was like a tiny diamond lost somewhere on a wooded path and, in fact, the world would not have missed it a bit.

I didn't go all the way to the top bench with a view to the south of sand quarries cut away, looking like giant chunks of marbled halavah sliced away. I stayed instead in a woodsy grove half way to the top and sat against a madrone tree moss-hairy from winter rains, and pulled out my pen.

When I got up, the creaky place in my hip joint shot with pain and I was unsteady, grabbing the hairy tree for balance. I am aging I have noticed. It is gradually creeping over me like fog—a pinched nerve here, a stiffness there. It is gradual so you won't one day wake up and think you are sick with something, your joints rusty as an iron gate. I shrugged it off, snapped my fanny pack back on, and continued my walk down through the oaks and madrones, over the sandy path at the bottom, and to my car.

I am writing about things that happened many years ago. Sometimes surprises are uncovered, like tiny bugs crawling out from under a rock, or flowers hiding under brush, so fragile and shy that only on looking closely, do I discover them. There are days when I want to gloss over things, get from this or that story onto the next, get this whole thing over with and let it finally rest in peace. If I get down on my hands and knees to look, I am afraid of opening a nest of biting ants or an army of scorpions. I don't want to look that closely. I want to laugh at all this. Yet some things will just never be funny, and laughing at them would make a lie of the past, like a grotesque clown wearing an eternal red smile while underneath he is a wino and a cad.

CHAPTER 14

Milton, The Psychic

"Reality is merely an illusion, albeit a very persistent one."

- Albert Einstein

When I met Tom, I didn't fully realize what a brilliant mind he had. Despite his love of science, the stacks of *Scientific American* he blazed through as if they were books of cartoons, his musical intellect—I found him a bit narrow and inflexible in his grasp of art or writing, or anything spiritual. He was authoritarian, obsessed with projects and process. When applied to finite projects like garden and backpacking trips, he was at peak brilliance.

But now, Tom was applying his engineering genius to the house, a project that was *not* finite. It was epochal—more a vision than a real-time venture. What was done so far was solid—the rock foundation, rounded sides, the girded strength of a castle. It needed only a drawbridge and a moat. Yet, the house was stuck in limbo, and his mind began to turn to other things—namely the whole rest of the universe.

He was smoking epicurean homegrown and he began to devour all the metaphysical books he could get his hands on: Edgar Cayce. Elizabeth Kubler Ross's books on death and dying, the books of Jane Roberts, channeled through her by Over-Soul Seth. In a matter of months the cosmos was zinging in his head where there had been a void. He could astral travel. He could escape the time warp of the half-built house. Go anywhere. But the great house could not.

It sat there like a strange shaped monolith from outer space, delivered there in the secret hour of some forgotten night. It was so big. What was it anyway? What would it be one hundred years from now? A chalet? A mountain inn? A ruin?

Oh, rain-warped house without walls
giant aircraft carrier afloat among the redwoods
You sit patient as a Buddha on the hill
watching the seasons roll by
Yet in winter I have seen you
shed long drips of tears
into pots and coffee cans and towels
in a symphony
of syncopated rain

I began to commiserate with the great hulk of the house that was defeated, abandoned and abused. I became the empathic mother figure crying along.

Around us, the world was in flux. The goats had babies again. New houses rose up around us. Our children climbed on school buses in the dark morning. The wheatgrasses grew tall. The thistles grew taller. The house was nestled in a time warp of a cocoon. There was a great sadness about it. It was turning inward, reclusive. The half-built house on the hill was having a mid-life crisis.

In the early days when Tom built the house model, he took it with him everywhere we visited. People gathered 'round when he lifted off the roof exposing the tiny steps, the rounded windows, the living room spoke wheel of beams. But over time the house model got knocked around, began to come apart, the wood splintered and ratty, and it eventually bit the dust. And the house plans? I lost track of them. I have no idea what could have happened. They disappeared as mysteriously as did the red down double-mummy sleeping bag.

I'm not sure whether the house took on the sickness of its master, or the other way around. Either way, Tom came to know that to fulfill his destiny, he was in need of healing.

In the backwoods of Vajrapani, Claire, an ex-nurse, learned the practice of Regenesis, energy work to open channels, revive hidden memories, release childhood pain. She did her work in a healing center in town.

Tom began to go to Claire twice a week. He found himself regressing to the traumatic memories of his infancy when he nearly died of an infection. Through her touch Claire was leading him one millimeter at a time through all the remembered and forgotten crises of his life, releasing locked emotions and triggering rebirth. He would cry like a baby, laugh, and come home flushed and raw. But with me, he was quiet, detached; he did not share himself. I watched him go away. I was left out—a petulant little girl.

He continued his ritual walks to town after the morning milking of the goats. Every day, five miles to town. Five miles back home. The walking man.

When a deep-sea diver reaches a critical depth he goes into nitrogen narcosis, and is compelled to go deeper and deeper despite the danger. When Tom reached the womb through Regenesis, he wanted to keep going. He called Milton, a psychic in Los Gatos: his specialization—past life regression.

Tom came back from his session with a tape that he played and replayed for many days. The tape revealed that he had been a powerful seer and innovator in other lives, but that it was his karmic problem to be unable to transmit his knowledge to others. This was his soul's great chronic frustration, and the repeating quest of his lifetimes.

He continued the dive in a self-induced narcosis, fathoms deeper, layer after layer, back into history, until he had worked out the whole genealogy of his past lives, as well as that of most of the people of Boulder Creek. The town was Atlantis reborn. We were all old Atlantis souls reinventing ourselves in 1980.

He got an ephemeris and studied the transits of planets and other astral bodies in relation to his moment of birth, and began to record his revelations as each celestial conjunction occurred. Then he began to develop a software program so that anyone could plug in their birthdate and access their own revelations at their astral conjunctions. But, mired so deep in his own psyche, he never finished this software program. Is this what Milton the psychic meant when he talked of Tom's karmic problem of failure to reach the masses? Did Milton really know?

He could put himself into a trance; he didn't need Milton anymore. He would sit with his headphones on listening to Schoenberg's *Transfigured Night,* and when a transit occurred the music would engender an altered state, and he would write down his revelations.

In his college days music had been a private thing. He went to the music lab every day at UC Berkeley to explore new pieces: Mahler, Berg, Satie. In our San Francisco days, music was a shared and evocative experience—every kind, from rock to jazz to classical. I had danced for him, rock music blasting from the space between the speakers in the Zone Called Paradise.

Now, he was taking music back again into his own private world. Headphones. Sanctified music. Transcendental escape. Astral traveling. The Music of the Spheres. One more way to shut out his family and the world.

He began to rattle on incessantly. He was a talking machine. Sitting cross-legged at the redwood round table rocking forward and backward like a crazed rabbi, churning up revelations, writing them down.

Sometimes as I walked around putting things away, running a bath, he followed after me, words reeling out of him, an endless monotone of revelation. He was a cerebrum that walked. I couldn't listen anymore. I couldn't get away from it.

Always on the periphery of my vision was the rocking. He sat at the center of our house, pumping up revelations like water from a well. And the pile of papers grew.

What must it have felt like, commiserates The White Raven, to be Tom—that desperate, that despondent—to know that he had miscalculated, that the house was a horrible mistake that could not be made right, that there was no way out of it but to wander the cosmos and live in past lives.

This was the heroic period of New Age therapies: Power Psychology. Wilhelm Reich said the body is a vehicle to the psyche: Gestalt Therapy, Bioenergetics, Primal Therapy. Rolfing that hurt. Descents to the Underworld where you would meet your boogiemen. And now Regenisis where the healer's hands could direct you back, back to your childhood, to your birth, and even to the womb.

But can you really deconstruct a man, take him back to the womb and then send him out into the real world where a ceiling is not a ceiling, and the rain comes pouring down onto the floor of his half-built house?

Can one jump off the operating table in the middle of surgery? Where was the "re" in Regenesis?; where was the healing? If a person is torn down, he must be rebuilt again, slowly, with work, over time. That is therapy. Otherwise, he may be left stripped and raw, on a fast track to oblivion.

CHAPTER 15

Pink Velour Shirt

TOM'S WALKING CHANGED. THE LONG smooth steady gait was of the old Tom who would plant his feet in front of the concrete mixer or the sawhorses, pulling nails from wood. Now he floated. He sprang up and down like a deer about to bound away. There was hardly enough gravity to hold him down.

Tom Corn was getting strange: his walk, his talk, even his clothes. In the San Francisco days he had bought his clothes from the Town Squire, the Polk Street store popular with gay men. He loved the colorful, psychedelic paisley patterns of the folk shirts with long, puffy sleeves. His favorite dress shirt was high-necked, deep blue, pure velvet. I wondered then why he had wanted to dress that way. I figured that it was the times, his love for good quality and the luxurious feel of soft fabrics. That he might be borderline gay did cross my mind, but I came to believe that it was rather his eccentric nature and his disregard for what others might think.

In the mountains when he was master builder of the house, he learned to swagger. He looked sexy in blue jeans, and his favorite pair—worn thin, soft, light blue—became iconic. I patched them when they tore until they were a collage of patches. Those pants were a sexy symbol of his manhood. Fancy blue velvet from the Town Squire was the furthest thing from his mind. It lived in the past right along with Lockheed Missiles and Space.

One day I made him a pair of drawstring pants, the only thing besides pillows I knew how to sew. He picked out fabric for his unisex pants—velour, colorful. After that, things got really strange. Ironically, as he became more inward, lost in his music and his revelations, he presented himself outwardly in a conspicuous, brazen way. He would rummage through the Goodwill outlet called the Bargain Barn where you could buy clothes by the pound. He would come home with an assortment of women's tops; I remember a short-sleeved tight pink shirt with an embroidered flower, in stretch velour. He got his ear pierced, wore an earring. When we went to his niece's high-tone wedding in San Francisco, he insisted on wearing such an outfit, would not listen to anyone. He was the weird uncle of the wedding.

Each morning Tom milked the goats. Each afternoon he walked to town smoking a joint. Each evening he milked the goats. This routine kept him on the earth, but not by much. I was the grounding rod, and without me he might have floated away into the blue Sierra.

After the rip-off, the secret plants in the grow room of the crawl space down below continued their tall, spindly growth under the hideous blue fluorescent lights, and were tricked into flowering when the light was cut a degree each day—stripped and harvested and bagged into green plastic garbage bags and dragged upstairs to be trimmed.

Until one day they came up the hill—two men with masks and rifles—and they stole all the bags while Tom and Ben stood watching, and they ran down the hill with their loot, whooping and shooting blanks into the air.

And the house grew quiet, resigned,
as did the Master,
and the hippie-happy days were done

CHAPTER 16

Mother's Day

MOTHERS DAY, 1981

It is the Saturday before Mothers Day. It is raining. I am waiting for him to come home. I start spaghetti to keep busy. How many scenes in our lives might have been different if the opening line had been different?

How different for us, if the house hadn't been leaking like a sieve when he walked in. How different if I had been standing, open arms, by a brick fireplace in the living room of a cozy warm house with spaghetti simmering on the stove.

This morning we had agreed that we would spend time together after his session with Claire, that we would have three hours alone before the kids got home from school.

I remember back to his first session with Claire when he returned excited and flushed. When they work together, she is a conduit, drawing out the boyhood fears, the monster outside the bedroom window. When he releases some childhood trauma she jumps as if an electric current had surged through her.

He does not trust me. I will take things wrong, so he protects his new and open face from me: the needy, sour, skeptical wife. I am jealous that she can love him in a rarefied atmosphere without ten years of rusty behavior patterns, without electric bills and dripping ceilings, burnt toast and morning breath.

1:30: The rain is falling hard now. When Tom left, he walked to town in a drizzle that he said was sure to blow over. I run around putting pans and cans under the leaks. The one in Ben's room is out of control. The plastic is torn above the ceiling and the rain pours into a twenty-five gallon container, the floor soaked from the splatter. I build a fire with what few scraps of wood we have left.

2:30: Tom is not here. The session would be two hours, he had said. He should have been back by 11:00.

3:00: The children will be home in one hour. I am worried that by the time he gets here I will not be able to hide my disappointment.

3:15: Footsteps on the stairs. He walks into the room and right past me. I say tentatively, "This is the storm that would blow over, ay?" He goes wordlessly into the back room and I hear, "My God Laurie, you have to stay on top of these leaks. What are you doing! Or are you just waiting for me to come home to fix it?"

He is yelling at me, about the house leaks. . . yelling at me! I walk back there and he is lying on the bed, a wounded expression on his face.

"Fuck it" I mutter, and go to find my raincoat. "I will take a walk." I write him a note:

"When the first thing you do is yell at me, how can we feel close? I'm sorry. I'm sorry for everything."

I grab my coat, run down the steps, and out into the cold rain. I walk to the Country Club. My pants are soaking, my tennis shoes are full. The rain frosts my hair. My skin is tingling. I sit for a few minutes on a tree stump at the Country Club, then start back. We will talk.

As I am nearing the final bend before China Grade, Tom streaks past me on the opposite side of the road. He walks on, ignoring me. I cross the street and start to follow him, saying feebly, "Oh, come on, Tom." No response. He keeps on walking. I stand in the street staring after him and yell, "The kids will be home from school soon. They're your kids too!"

I walk on, thinking, A man can have the luxury of walking to town while the mother has to hurry home because the kids are coming home from school. I have to schedule my angry walks between the school buses. At home, I watch Ben and Sami walk up the hill. Sami is wailing. "What's the matter, sweetie?"

"I fell in the grass and I peed in my pants, and here's your Mother's Day presents," she cries. And if I hadn't been home, I am thinking.

They take off their wet clothes. I heat water for the tub, get in with Sami while Ben stays in the kitchen drawing airplanes. After the bath, they present me with their gifts. Ben's is a watercolor of airplanes and a big paper with "MOTHER" in the middle, and along the sides: "Mom, you're the best. Oh, you're the best. That's what I call a great mom. Hey, you're great, mom. Excellent special mom."

Sami gives me a kindergarten recipe book written by the children. "Thank you," I say. "I love my presents."

5:00: I am waiting. I am thinking, This coming Tuesday in writing class I'll be reading this story. It will have an ending by then. *But now I am worried. When he left he wouldn't speak to me. . . and the look on his face when he lay in bed. I go to the phone to call Claire. Her answering service picks it up. I am annoyed. Four and a half hours he spends with her, and I can't even get through to her.*

6:00: I reach Claire and ask her what happened.

"He didn't tell you about it?"

"No, we haven't talked at all. In fact, we had a fight and he's gone. That's the way it's been around here lately."

"Tom did incredibly deep work today. Three-and-a-half hours. I had to go to sleep afterward, I was so drained. He had a spontaneous rebirthing. I drove him home so he wouldn't have to deal with buses and all. He really had a conscious desire to share it with you while he was still in that space."

"Then why did he walk into the house and start criticizing me? It completely threw me."

"When he left the car he was in a very soft place. Something must have happened between the car and the house."

"Yes. . . me. He doesn't feel safe with me. He is much more drawn to you than to me these days."

"He is drawn to himself, and he gets there through me. We need to talk."

Why didn't I come to him on the bed instead of writing him an angry note? But I didn't, and now he is gone and the last words from me on the road were screaming sarcasm. When will he return? Maybe tomorrow, maybe never. We do what we do. . . and we are not saints.

7:00: "Let's take a walk, " I say to the children. The rain has stopped. It's as wet inside as it is out. "Let's take a walk." So I leave him a second note reading:

"I spoke to Claire. She told me you wanted to come home to be with me. I so wish that you had shown me that. Maybe unconsciously you didn't really want to share it. I spent all morning changing pails and if I missed a few, it will not matter. The house gets wet. The house gets wet. In any case, just know that I am here for you. I wish you would come home. This time of healing will probably not be smooth for us. We need to talk more. We need to spend some time together. I love you, Laurie."

We walk to Alexandra's house up Memory Lane. I hadn't seen her in ages since she had become a community college instructor in Women's Studies. She is showing movies. Sami and Ben settle in to stay, so I walk home feeling blessed with this precious time. Tom will read my note when he returns, and we'll have some time alone.

I walk in and see my note untouched on the table. The house is desolate, rugs stinking of plastic rainwater. It is cold and I am shivering. I can't stay and wait. It is twilight and I start out, again, toward the Country Club. How many more walks will I take before this night is over? I walk beyond the Country Club to the bridge. It grows dark. I watch for a tall figure on the opposite side of the road. I give up and walk back home.

The children are back now. Sami falls asleep on the sofa because her bed is wet. Where is Tom? Claire has not heard from him. She has called twice. She is concerned. There is nothing I can do. I have no car. It is 2:00 a.m. and I am at the typewriter, waiting. . .

Limbo. . .Are you left with feelings of outrage? How painful. Yet only one side of the story is known. When the other side of the story is taking a walk, it gets left out. If he expects to be loved in this story then he must make an appearance. He must make contact.

3:00 a.m: I am thinking that maybe he is spending the night in his grandfather's old Ford Falcon down by the goat house. It is a dark night and I walk blindly down the driveway, my feet scraping through the brush. I peer into the Falcon. He is not there. I check the broken-down VW, then the truck. And what would I have done if he had been there?

The Next Day. . .

5:00a.m: I go to bed exhausted. At 7:30 I awake with a start. The goats! I forgot to feed the goats last night. They are pregnant. They have to have their oats. I walk down the wet path. Their water basins are almost full. I check the feeders for alfalfa. They are full too. I notice Tom's knit cap there on the floor, the hat he was wearing when he walked away. It is damp. He was back here. Did he come when we were at Alexandra's? Did he read my note? Or did he just sneak home to feed the goats?

When I get back to the garage, I notice that the boxes of old rags by the refrigerator are emptied and their contents strewn around. Tom had been here too. Later that morning I see that the milk is gone from the refrigerator.

To the children it is just another Saturday with Saturday morning cartoons. They ask where Dad is and I explain, "Daddy goes to therapy at Claire's house. Therapy means that she is helping him remember things from when he was a boy. Daddy needs time alone to think. He will be home later."

Claire calls and says, "Tom's not home yet?"

"No," I say. I'm scared for him."

I call Alexandra: "Have you seen Tom at all . . . since yesterday?

"I saw him walking in the rain yesterday afternoon, almost to town. He was drenched. He was just walking along smoking a joint—looked all right to me."

I make lunch for the children, clean the house. I strip the rooms of all the wet rugs and the foam padding underneath. I throw the rugs out onto the deck, our future living room, and make a decision. I will not bring these dirty, smelly, rain-soaked rugs back into our house. I will buy indoor-outdoor carpeting. I gather the wet clothing from Ben's drawers, hang them outside, let the sun do its work. Standing there on the deck hanging out the clothes, I feel the sun on my face, and realize that sometimes The Big Eye is my friend.

About 4:00, Alexandra calls me and reports, "Tom is on his way home. I saw him walking this way. He's about as far as Bracken Brae now." My heart jumps. I put the spaghetti on low. An hour passes and he hasn't arrived yet. At 5:30 I tell the children I am going for a short walk. As I round the bend on Big Basin, I see him on the opposite side of the road—in exactly the same spot where we parted yesterday. I cross over and say, "Well, want to try that scene again?"

"No," he says flatly.

"What's that?" referring to the white plastic bucket he is carrying.

"Just a container I found in the Country Club garbage bin. It's full of grease, but there are things I can use it for." We walk home together in silence.

"Do you want some spaghetti?"

"Sure, I'm starving." he says.

"Did you sleep at Omland last night?"

"No, too many people there. I slept in the goat house. I figured you wouldn't remember to feed them." He came home to sleep with his precious goats who could never do him wrong. He slept on a pile of straw and covered himself with the rags from the garage.

"I never thought of the goat house."

"I know. I heard you opening the cars in the middle of the night. I even came into the house late at night to get my jacket. You were sitting at the typewriter and didn't notice. In fact, you walked right by me this morning when you went down to the goat house. I was sitting on top of the welder in the garage."

"I'm tired. I'm going to bed," he says.

After putting the children to bed I crawl into ours. Tom is lying on his side facing me. I lie down with my back to him. He runs his hand over my buttocks. Then he is sleeping. I am desolate, alone. How can he fall asleep like a child without a word of connection? My mind is wild and racing hour after hour, and finally I take my pillow and get into bed with Sami.

Mothers Day. I awaken early and return to our bed. Tom lies staring at the ceiling. I get up and walk into the kitchen. All that morning we pass each other in the house, but there are no words. I gather laundry. I will go to the laundromat, take the children with me and leave him to his marijuana and his friends, the goats, and his childish silence and his rain-warped castle on the hill.

I gather no more than I can carry in the backpack. It is drizzling, and we wait for the shuttle bus on Big Basin Way. I can see our house from the bus stop, plastic windows glistening wet in the sun. It looks sad. We wait, the children playing in the puddles. Apparently we have missed the bus, and Ben is coughing and his shoes are wet. "Let's go home," I say. "We'll do laundry another time."

When I enter the house Tom is on the phone. I hear him saying, "Mom's not home?. . .To say Happy Mother's Day. I'll call later."

Mother's Day? I had forgotten all about it. I get a flash of Mother's Day when I was a kid, when we would serve my Mom breakfast in bed and shower her with presents. I slump down on the sofa. Tom seems a bit brighter now, but I am drained.

He sits at the table listening to music, his headphones on. The children are playing around him. He flips off the radio, rests his head in his hands, his eyes closed. In a guttural voice, he orders the children to leave the room. They continue to buzz around him, playing a game. He picks up a toy and throws it in Sami's direction, hollering, "Get out of here. Now! I have to be alone." She runs, and I hear her frightened sobbing in the back room.

And then it begins—a repetitive wail, a sound not human, more than human: the baying of a feral beast, the howl of a wolf, the plaintive call of a lonely soul reaching for connection. His hand is shaking, convulsing as an old man's. . .

"You have to move," he cries. "I have to lie down. I need some blankets. So cold." I go to the back to gather the blankets from our bed. Sami and Ben stand there waiting and listening. I say to them, "Daddy will be all right now. Do you remember when I told you about the therapy he's doing? He is learning how to cry."

"But what is he crying about?" Sami asks.

"He is crying for all the times when he was your age that he wanted to cry, but stopped himself. And when he gets done crying he will feel better."

"But he didn't have to hurt my feelings." wails Sami in a new outburst of passion.

"I know, sweetheart. He didn't want to hurt your feelings. He just couldn't help it then."

Tom is lying face down on the floor. With a down jacket on and four heavy comforters, he is shivering. I sit next to him and begin to lightly rub his back. He cries softly for a long while, sometimes laughing, sometimes sobbing. . . but calmer now. He says, "Tell the kids to come in here." I call them. They sit silently. Sami gets her coloring book, sprawls out on her stomach and begins to color. When Tom asks for some tissue to blow his nose, she runs to get it and returns to her place by his side. It is Mother's Day.

A moving story, whispers The White Raven. I read it to my writing group, Ellen Bass deeply sighing, as she was wont to do. While Tom was purging himself, there was no place for another person in the room except to console, to bring tissues, to stay out of the way. This, ever and again, was all about him. The crying little boy, the lost creature wailing for connection.

And what was I really feeling? Be honest, nudges The Raven. I was scared for him, but was I such a saint that I did not feel left out, used, a trifle resentful? When did I get to have my breakdown? My walk-about? Where was my freak out? Where was my Out? I was a saint maybe, but I was an angry saint.

CHAPTER 17

Soul Mate

It was early evening. The children were at Alexandra's. Tom sat at the table writing and listening to Schoenberg with headphones on. Tears were rolling down his face.

"Lenore was my soul mate in all my other lives. That explains everything. I know I mean more to her than she'll admit. But her soul knows."

I sat down across from him. "And who was I? What part do you have for me? Why does she get the leading role? What was I to you?"

He waited until I was through. "I wanted to tell you that. It came to me that in primordial times you were an earth mother. And I was with you then. We were always together in that way. We have not connected much over our lifetimes, but it was always with passion. We bring that out in each other."

She was my husband's soul mate? And I, his love slave? His passion whore? How could I compete with centuries where she was the one? The love he couldn't have, the one who was there hovering through the ages, around the stone wall, through the castle window, across the English meadow—the Eternal Other Woman. I began to protest, to ask questions. He rose from the table, picked up the pail at the top of the steps and walked down, down the hill to milk the goats. He would be safe down there. No one to argue with him. No petulant remarks. He walked casually down the hill, swinging his pail, to milk the goats.

But my mind was swirling with anger and arguments that I would sling at him when he returned up the steps. And when he walked back in, I opened my mouth and began, and he said, "Are you still stewing about that?" And I shut up, shut down. What was the use?

I saw my mother and father standing in the hallways of my mind in a soft embrace. I knew that out there was a world that was right and true, and I was mired deep in a world that was dark and wrong. My mother and father stand locked in that embrace for all time. It was not until I heard the words 'soul mate' that I understood that that is what they were. The fact of their union gives power and credence to the word, and there is a certain beauty in that.

But there is danger when a word gives power and credence to a thing. Words can give rise to an idea that becomes a belief that takes on a life of its own. Not only had Other Woman come. She had brought with her all lives past. The words 'soul mate' gave rise to a myth and I was left on a road shrinking into the distance, living in the humble fact of our marriage.

I am sad today
but not afraid
I feel the end coming close
to the marrow of my soul

I will not forget
The perfect moments
are embedded safe
like deeply colored jewels
the light turning ever inward on itself
  a snowy world of alpine meadows
  and big Montana sky
  cool morning lakes
  picking huckleberries
  alone together
  I will remember

CHAPTER 18

If . . .

If there had been no house. . .

Isn't it possible, asks the White Raven, that we might have lasted if there had been no house? Tom was not a bad man, just driven, and self-absorbed, and in the end, scared and desperate.

If there had been no house. . .maybe he would have found other projects to throw himself into—organic gardening, or cooking, or the ephemeris software he had conceived that brings revelations to the user. We might have designed, together, a cozy small dwelling and lived as a family in The Comfort Zone. We might have been more attentive parents. We might have tried harder. We might have matured through his "anima lust" and my tendency to be submissive and secretive and afraid to communicate.

There will never be a way to know this. The saga of the half-built house is the only one I have, and lord knows, I have tried to be fair to both of us in this telling.

I have been reviewing this book and have discovered what feels like the heart of it. I was browsing through some ancient writings, all in their little Microsoft Word files, and I opened the original book of poems written in the 70s. There it was, the love—the physical, romantic, tender and persistent love between me and this man. I never stopped loving him even when I hated him, and it was likewise for him. In that way, we really were a match. You see, Tom, how this writing reveals my love, our love? I really did love you— fiercely, woefully, addictively. It is all here in these pages.

Also, dear reader, maybe, just maybe Tom could be given some kindness for daring to think he could build this magnificent dream house for his family, with speakers built into the wall, a heated slate floor, a rounded view of the mountains, and terraced gardens. If there was one thing about him that was consistent and true, it was his love of quality. His speakers were state of the art. His music collection, robust and full. He had the complete piano works of Rachmaninoff played by the master himself. And let's not leave me out—I was, I venture to say, the highest quality woman he could have found.

Maybe he had an edifice complex, but would I have recognized him if he had designed some simple A-frame just because it was efficient and affordable? His vision held him to the project until it could no more, and the half-built house became the great, sad failure of his earthly life.

So, right in the middle of all this confusion and despair, I dedicate this poem to the ever-present, suffering, smoldering, and abiding love.

As I walk up the path of our hill
I breathe in spring
orange poppies dot the field
first of the season
Tom is up the hill working the terrace for a garden
smoothing the soil,
raking out rocks and tossing them into the wheelbarrow
He moves with grace
his back already tanning
By June his hair will be waves of gold

When I reach the terrace
he drops his rake and follows me up to the house
There is that awkward quiet
when we are home alone,
that unspoken, teasing question
of whether we will go to bed
or just go on with our day
like new lovers pretending
we don't know what is about to happen

We fall into the waterbed laughing
I have ridden these waves so many times
Across the road
the whirring of a rototiller
cars on China Grade
people going about their day
and here am I, in this love affair
our bedroom ringing
with the colors of late afternoon
his face jumping with pink
and his curls as gold as June

CHAPTER 19

Tuna Fish Rebellion

Does the realization of the absurd require suicide?
Camus answers: "No. It requires revolt."

FOR SOME REASON I ALWAYS carried this vision of perfect motherhood: The day is bright, glittering. There is a luminous green lawn in front of a large suburban house. I am slim and trim in blue jeans, squatting, a ball in my hands, ready to throw it to my little toddler boy.

One day I woke up with an idea. A family outing. I pictured packing a lunch and going to Highlands Park in Ben Lomond, sitting on the green, throwing a ball around—just the four of us. I couldn't remember if we had ever done such a thing, and it was about time that we did one normal thing as a family. I told Tom my idea, and he answered a bit sheepishly that he was on his way to visit Lenore that afternoon. As he started off, sauntering down the driveway, I picked up a chair and threw it at him.

I WOULD HAVE TOLD YOU I WAS RUNNING AWAY BUT I WANTED TO SURPRISE YOU

I have run away. This morning while Joni Mitchell was singin' "Blue" I was packin' my stuff in a brown grocery bag. I planned to get a motel and type all day, see how it felt to run away, write a poem by the ocean at sunset, come home in the morning—GET OUT OF BOULDER CREEK. You were in town buying B12 for the plants. I would leave when you returned, and I would not say where I was going.

I thought about how you ran away last month…just took off down the road in the rain in your beat up down jacket and knit cap and your torn-up tennis shoes… left without a word, without a hint, and never showed up 'til the next evening.

While I was waiting to run away I was chopping vegetables for Beef Bourgignon. There was just time to get it in the pot before you returned from town.

"The stew is in the pot," I said. "All you have to do is thicken the sauce tonight. I won't be here."

"Smells good," was your reply. "Uh…will you cut my hair before you go?" So you took a bath while I watered the garden, and I cut your hair out on the deck, watching your golden curls lift away on the breeze.

I was already worried about the children. What would they think? What will you tell them? When you left, they didn't ask. Maybe they didn't even notice. I am already worried that they will put on dirty clothes tomorrow for school, that they'll go off with soiled hands and faces, that Sami won't get her medicine. I'm already thinking that maybe I'll be home by 6:00 a.m.—just to make sure. I don't know how mothers run away.

Early this morning Sami typed me a note: "Dear Mom, I love you very much. I hope you love me too." and Ben… Ben has given me a thistle weed with purple flowers in a hand-made carton held together with tape. It was as if they knew my secret plan.

"Will you take me to town with you, Mommy?" Sami asked.

"Tomorrow, Sami, tomorrow I will buy you some sandals and skirts for the summer. Now I have to go alone."

I am in the restaurant-bar of the Dream Inn, fancy beachside hotel near the Boardwalk. The sun is setting and I am sitting here alone. It is happy hour. Things are beginning to liven up as pretty young women and out-of-town businessmen hook up at the bar. The pheromones in the bar zone are almost visible.

I am not feeling free. Not attractive. Not available. Not anything different from what I was before I left home, except that now I am lonely. The waitress hands me a menu. I choose a tuna sandwich. I have run away. A lonely table in a beach-fancy hotel with a tuna sandwich and a coffee.

The great tuna fish rebellion.

My heart was trembling. I never remembered being angry as a child. I used to think that I was born without anger. Two days ago, I had thrown a chair at my husband. Yesterday I had run away.

I saw Charles, now an established healer, in Coffeetopia, and sat down with him. "I need help. I'm so angry I can't sleep. I need a tune-up."

"I'll order the parts," he said gently, putting his hand on mine. "Come to my office at 3:00 tomorrow."

I lay on the table and he put on new age music and lit incense. He began speaking softly. He touched my temples. He touched my feet. With the heat of his hands he moved through the *chakras* of my body. At first I felt a tingling in my fingers, like the fizz of ginger ale. It moved through my hands up my arms until they were surging with an electric current. The *chi* moved through me, from my feet up my legs and finally my whole body was immobilized and I felt as if I were suspended above the table, charged by a bolt of pure electricity.

"I'm scared. It's too strong. I can't move at all."

"You are fine. Just go with it. It will bring release. When it's over, you will be different."

When the *chi* stopped moving, I felt that all the anger that had been holding me frozen had been dispersed through me like a warm shower of sparks—like shock therapy, but with my own electrical energy supplying the shock.

"Your heart *chakra* is open again. Take your time and don't get down off the table until you're ready. You have had a profound healing. You may never be the same."

That was more than a healing. That was a teaching. Anger becoming its opposite—compassion? It makes sense, because in anger there is much passion, much heart.

Compassion. Yes. I can forgive him all the mistakes, says The White Raven, but I cannot forgive what he told his daughter twenty years later. He told her that those days of his metaphysical wanderings and revelations were the peak days of his life.

Peak days that were always and forever about him—his wife and children, always and forever, the collateral damage.

A father and mother sit in a restaurant
eating pancakes
They are in animated discussion
Over the mother's shoulder is slung a newborn babe
She balances the baby girl as she eats
The baby begins to squirm
The father's arms reach out to take the baby
The mother eats
The baby fusses
The father does not give her back
The mother hands him a bottle
They are talking all the while

It may not seem that this could be a poem
this conversation: the passing of baby
from mother to father
his arms outstretched
reaching for the baby. . . without being asked
without even being asked. . .

PART 6

On This Hill A Buddhist Lives

In this life
there is nothing
you can call your own.
Even your umbilical cord
was only on loan

- Laurie Corn

I love these sounds
tinking of a spoon against a cup
bleating of the goat
hum of the car coming home

I made a cake this afternoon
When I poured brown sugar for the frosting
a mob of ants scurried out in all directions
I spread the sugar in a plate
They left me just enough—two thirds cup

Forgive me, Mom,
We have learned to share our home with
field mice in the shelves
scorpions in the garage
baby frogs on the kitchen sink
bees, bats and flies
and ants in the sugar
But they have left me just enough
keeping the sugar loose
as earthworms keep the garden

It is fly season again

but I have become a Buddhist on this hill
and when I see a fly drowning in some apple juice
I fish it out to drag its wings dry

I could sit here for hours at the top of the hill
listening to the wind
the laughter of men down below
        throwing horseshoes
gazing at the sculpture of stark white clouds
against the deep blue infinite sky

CHAPTER 1

My Life Work

In the months to come I spent many hours at Trina's log house in the trees behind us—trimming pot, drinking espresso and talking about past lives, talking about what was happening to my husband. One night I returned home to the strangest trip of my life.

I stood there at the threshold of a living room with rug walls. In the corner is an old cook stove hooked up to a five-gallon propane tank. The windows are torn plastic. Cheap flowered curtains cover shelves beside the stove. A man, my husband, in a brown down jacket patched with silver duct tape, sits on the floor and he is rocking forward and backward, headphones on; his forehead is churning, his eyebrows conducting music. He begins to look quieter to me. His face widens and his eyes appear slanted. He is a Chinese elder.

I couldn't stand how lately when he was in a trance I felt queasy, afraid that I was getting drawn into the magnetic field of craziness surrounding him. So I broke into his trance and blurted out, "By the way, something's been bothering me. If you were all these powerful people in your past lives, I must have been somebody along the way too, other than just Earth Mother, or else why would you be hanging out with me?"

"Who do you think you were?"

"Van Gogh," I volunteered, tongue-in-cheek.

"Keep going—what makes you think so?"

"Because sometimes I wake up in the night with a mad desire to cut off my ear!!"

"Are you drawn to his work?" he continued.

"Yes. No. Not as much as Cezanne and Gauguin and Matisse. I love the emotion, the color, the strong forms. I don't care for his early drawings."

"It's just like you to be so critical of your own work."

For the next few weeks a strange series of events unfolded, starting with the day I happened upon a copy in the thrift shop of *Dear Theo,* the letters between Van Gogh and his brother Theo. That night I began to read the letters. On every other page I got the chills. He loved the same French books as I. He tried teaching as a young man and failed at it miserably, as did I. And then I read that his favorite pencil for drawing was the carpenter's pencil. That was too much. I always choose the carpenter's pencil over the new fancy graphite sticks.

I was looking through one of my Van Gogh art books and discovered on the inside cover a black and white ink drawing of an olive orchard. It was remarkably similar to a drawing I had done once in the hills of Judea surrounding Jerusalem—the placement of the trees, the line work, the vitality. I was just sitting in that orchard by myself with a sketchbook when an actual shepherd wandered by leading a flock of sheep. Something timeless came over me; I took the pencil and this energetic drawing of the old twisted olive trees just drew itself.

I came to understand what was driving Tom. And to think that he was spending all day at it—weaving together the past-life web of all the people he knew. What others might call a psychotic break or drug-induced hallucination, he knew as transcendental experience, and in his expanded consciousness he saw me dwindling into the distance, tethered to the mere ground.

He said that he was moving too far and too fast for me. Sometimes I envied him that he could wander away and see universes folding in on themselves, and then come to dinner. I wanted a glimpse of it, but Earth Woman is happiest with her size eleven feet planted firmly on the ground. I was happy enough flying in my dreams.

Some nights I would sit out on the living room deck looking at the sky that was its ceiling, searching the stars that were his stars.

I love you in my memory of you, but I don't know you anymore.
Sometimes you go so far away I'm afraid you won't come back.
You are Don Quixote and she is your Dulcinea.
and you are a stranger in our house.

He could see beyond this planet, beyond this life, but he could not see what was in front of him. . . and the house didn't matter and the children didn't matter, and we were losing him day by day.

I called Milton, the past-life psychic. "Milton," I said, "I need help. It's about Tom." Milton told me to come.

He answered the door and laughed, "I didn't picture you so tall."

A psychic, I said to myself.

He was very short, a little avuncular-looking man whose face was a lot like George Washington. We sat down and he went into a trance and said, "You are a passionately creative woman."

He's telling me what I want to hear, I thought. I said, "I don't really need to talk about myself. I'm here because I'm worried about Tom. He's putting himself in a trance every day and it's obvious to him, from what you said, that he was a powerful prophetic person in all of his past lives. I'm afraid for him, that he'll wind up on a street corner telling everyone he's Jesus."

"Before we can talk about Tom or about you and Tom, we need to see who you are."

He went into a deeper trance and said, "Your work in this life is to learn to be with a man without being dependent on him and without his being dependent on you."

"That is my life work?"

"Yes, you will see that it is, and as for your future life with Tom, I am not getting a clear picture. He has work to do alone. Be careful."

He told me my life work, and I left, seventy dollars poorer.

CHAPTER 2

Coffeetopia

Boulder Creek – Looking Back, 1998

This cafe used to be Simoni's Bar in the 70s, then a hair salon, now a spacious coffee shop with a tall redwood tree growing right through the ceiling in the middle of the room. Christmas lights are strung up and down the part of the tree that exits the building, and from the opposite end of town it looks like a huge lit-up dill pickle spearing the night sky.

When we moved here this was a funky little town with Jack's General Store at the center selling mud boots and raincoats and wool socks. Now Jack's is a gift shop with elegant pottery and juried art shows. Mac's 100 year Old Place is still there. The old western storefronts remain, but the insides keep changing all the time. The three-block long main street is full of tourist shops: jewelry, leather-made goods, a desk-top publishing house, and trendy coffee shops such as this.

I didn't know whether it was safe to come back to Boulder Creek to write. So much of my history here—twenty-five years: a marriage, a half-built house, two children—in short all of the 70s and some of the 80s reverberating in this tiny mountain town that is barely on the map. I picked a window table overlooking the creek, swollen with winter rains.

I am invisible here, a ghost among these newcomers, knowing what I know. The newcomers are part of the bedroom community that has settled, people who commute over the hill to San Jose's Silicon Valley and who have chosen to dwell "in the mountains." But they are not really in the mountains. They drop off their dry cleaning before work, shop for food after work, and retreat to their million dollar homes in the hills above the town.

To simplify—that was not necessarily our purpose, but it was the consequence of our choice to live in the mountains. And with simplifying is a trade-off. You can renounce the crazy, rat-race work-a-day world, but you might end up living in a trailer or a half-built house held together by duct tape and old rugs. You might end up with dirty kids whose most cherished gift is a new box of crayons. Your day might be the logistics of getting to the village laundry in the rain without a car and a backpack full of wet laundry, or shoveling dirt to keep the driveway from washing away, or emptying buckets and pots during the rains so the floor won't stink of water rot.

But survival stuff was still better for the soul than commuting on Highway 17 to Silicon Valley. Survival stuff kept you rooted to the rhythms of life, and looking back, even though I dreamed the dream of a washer-dryer, hot water, central heating and wooden cabinets in the kitchen—i.e. The Comfort Zone—I do now, and will always measure simplicity by those days. To keep that kind of simplicity nowadays, you have to work hard at it, saying "no" to this or that meeting, "no" to social engagements, "no" to the job that kills your spirit, and in the end when everyone thinks you are a recluse, you can say "Good. I have done it. It is a start."

And how did my kids fare, having grown up in this counterculture life? I want to talk about them. I have never been one to brag about my kids. People who do that annoy me. But in truth most of the kids I know from that era have a stamp of quirky greatness about them. Those years in the mountains were vintage years for the fruit of our loins.

Last year while sitting with Sami in Cafe Brazil in Santa Cruz, a young svelte waitress approached wearing chunky fashion heels, a short skirt revealing long, curvy legs, swinging hair and dangling earrings. She and Sami recognized each other and chatted about college majors and the future. When she left our table Sami said, "You probably know her parents, Bernie and Marie. They live up the Omland Road and make jewelry."

"Really!" I said. "Tamar used to house-sit their cabin when they were away. It was the cutest hippie cabin. I remember they had a lot of kids running around."

When the waitress returned I said, "I know your folks. They're good people. You and Sami were little hippie girls back then," as if to applaud their common heritage. Sami and she looked at each other and Sami said: "We were hippie kids, but we didn't exactly choose it."

If a character resume were written about Sami, it could read: She has the integrity and fierce independence of Gloria Steinem or Golda Meier, the aesthetic eye of Georgia O'Keefe, the openness of the prairie. She is dependable as the ocean, steady as a redwood, fun and playful as a chimpanzee with faces to match.

She took on the burden, all too young, of an independent thinker who took charge of her life. At age six she organized her own birthday party, picking out the invitations, writing in the time and place, mailing them. Was it that she loved being in charge, or was it that she didn't trust that her hippie mom would handle things? She always loved making lists—no doubt, she learned that one from me— and filling out applications. She was drawn to adding machines and offices, the machinery of the real world, as if preparing herself for a life that would be better than the one handed to her on a tin platter.

She has the sense of fairness innate to the Libra, and her Libra translates well into her art in an exquisite balance of space and color. She is a writer of raw and no-nonsense poetry and prose. She is a fountain of talent. She is my daughter. She is, at times, my grandmother. She is also my ally in this world.

When you have two kids and they are as different as bird and zebra, you know you are not meant to take credit or blame. Ben walks the earth in a tender way, like a fawn, like St. Francis. When he was small he loved plants and trees so much that he had names for all of them. There was a purple thistle down by the switchback of the driveway that he called "my favorite plant," and he always worried that a car might crush it.

He understood the ways of the planet in an intrinsic way; he could feel them. You could plant him in the middle of a forest and he would find his way, searching the sky and the direction of mountains, knowing the wind and light.

Once up at Omland, Tamar's hippie friend named Evening Star asked Ben, "Where do you come from, lad?"

Ben turned and pointed up at the starlit sky and said, "There, that one."

"I thought so," said Evening Star, smiling.

School was a torture for him. They spoke a language that he did not speak or comprehend. What did a science movie on weather mean to one who could look up at the formation of clouds and predict the weather for the next three days? His brain had too much integrity to memorize formulas in math when he had the answers by reaching for them in a conceptual place.

At age seven in New York City, overwhelmed by the skyscrapers and the weight of all that concrete on the earth, he said out of nowhere: "If gravity keeps pushing on the earth isn't the earth getting smaller and smaller?" Is that not the theory of the Black Hole?

Nowadays they have special classes and schools for kids like Ben who learn differently: kids with left-handed syndrome, ADHD, dysgraphia, Asperger's Syndrome. Back then they called him a slow learner; they tried to tame the festering stew of children by adding Ritalin to the diet of the special ones—so that kids like Ben could handle school and go mainstream.

I'm glad I left him alone. He has found his own way out of the forest, or into it perhaps, and the world is better off for him.

But enough. People who brag about their kids annoy me.

CHAPTER 3

Sami Bird

"Birds have wings so they can fly."

- Sami Bird – Age 7

She stood on the chair next to the stove
stirring marshmallows into butter
Mother and daughter in the kitchen
stirring and mixing, like some picture
out of Family Circle

I looked out the window
and saw a tiny bird light on the branch of a pear tree
"Oh Sam," I sighed, "I wish I were a bird"

She stopped her stirring and stared at me
"But then you couldn't be my mommy"
"Oh yes, sweetie, I could. You would be my little bird"
"But then we couldn't be making marshmallow crispies"
she sang
she sang

THIS STORY IS FOR YOU, little Sami. You are the star of it, almost the tragic heroine. Since those days of your illness I have had recurring dreams of your death—a circle of friends dancing around you and myself draped over your still warm body.

As it turns out you were not critically ill, but the fear inspired by the doctors, the hospitals, and long words like Idopathic Thrombocytapenia Purpura can terrorize a helpless mother waiting for answers. It began with the dark purple bruises spreading like ink under your skin. At first I thought you were getting hurt at school. The teachers at school thought you were getting hurt at home. When the bruises began to rise like welts under the spreading purple I took you to the doctor. He drew blood and had a sample rushed off by express car to the nearest lab.

He called late that evening and said that your blood contained zero platelets. Without platelets, bruises under the skin do not coagulate and heal. He advised me to take you to Stanford Children's Hospital immediately, because if you were to fall or hit your head you might bleed internally with damage to brain or spine. "In the middle of the night?" I asked. "Couldn't we go in the morning? She's safe in bed now."

"If it were my daughter, I would go now," he said. What he didn't understand is that in our "rustic" life style at the top of a hill, it was more dangerous to move you than to let you sleep. What he didn't know was that I had lent our old Ford Falcon to a woman across the street earlier in the evening and that it wasn't until 11:00 that she returned.

But I kept hearing "if it were my daughter..." and I decided to get you to the safety of the hospital even though the way to Palo Alto was up and down dark, twisting mountain roads. I gathered your pajamas and clothes and could not waken you from your sleep. Your father could not get caught up in the emergency of the scene, did not understand this need to move you in the middle of the night. He did not, could not get up from his floor place where he sat rocking.

And so I wrapped you in a blanket and carried you down the hill in the dark to the car at the bottom—terrified that I might trip. I tucked you in the back seat and drove up Highway 9 and down the steep and winding road to Woodside, and at 2:00 a.m. arrived at Stanford emergency entrance where a team of technicians was expecting us.

You were so brave. They told you they had to draw blood, the first of many times—and you held out your arm and never cried. At 3:00 in the morning a young doctor came to me and said:

"There are several possibilities. It may be ITP, but we haven't ruled out bone cancer or leukemia. We want to do a bone marrow check. This is a painful procedure." I stood to the side while the blood people were prepping you.

"We have to draw blood from deep in the hip marrow," they explained. The needle was huge. Sami, you were so determined to be brave, but when they drove in that needle you let out a wail from the depths of your being. While waiting for the results, I was invited to sleep in a room with cots. There I found other parents spending the night, some maybe knowing already what was in store for them. *Sleep?* I said to myself. *She may have bone cancer—and I am invited to sleep on a cot?*

The Universe must shudder when a parent loses a child. I thought of your babysitting friend, Lucy, a blond ethereal sprite who attracted birds when she sat on our hill and played the flute. She died at fifteen in a house fire while trying to save a friend. Charles called her a "fast runner." In her short life she was vegetarian, yogi, and friend to animals and people of all ages. Little Sami, are you a fast-runner too?

In the morning the doctors told me that you did not have a life-threatening disease. But your ITP was serious enough to warrant a transfusion of blood. When your platelet count was at a low normal they would release you.

You stayed for two weeks. You were like proud Madeline after her appendectomy. You felt better than most of the other children—energetic and happy. I would come to visit you and find you in the playroom bouncing balls with other kids who were bald from chemo. Compared to life in the half-built house this ward was like a luxury hotel, and I watched how pleased you were with your clean, warm accommodations.

The best part was the meals. They would bring you a menu in the morning on which you would check the items of your choice for that day.

I arrived one day just as you were preparing to eat. You sat in your bed like a royal princess, lifted the lid off the platter revealing the dinner of your choice and you exclaimed, "This is much better than the food at home." The mother of the little boy in the next bed raised her eyebrows and said, "Are you going to disown her?" And we had a good laugh.

You came home with more platelets than you had going in, kept the hospital menus in a drawer for a long time, wore a helmet in PE at school for the rest of the year, and although we continued our follow-up visits to Stanford for many months, we stopped when they began recommending the removal of your spleen because a splenectomy seems to cure chronic ITP.

Instead we went to visit Ed Jarvis in Pacific Grove. He was a tall, handsome, charismatic healer in the guise of chiropractor. He was Tamar's and Charles's doctor from their Big Sur days. Dr. Jarvis moved his fingers up and down your back, confirmed that your spleen was malfunctioning and said he was pretty sure he could get things going in the right direction by gentle manipulation.

Within a month your platelets were having platelets, multiplying like rabbits. On our last visit to Stanford I told the doctors of your miracle recovery under the hands of this New Age healer. They looked at each other, and I knew it was time to make our exit.

I learned from this event: that you are a truly brave soul and a survivor; what it could feel like to lose a precious child; that Tom could not be counted on; that traditional doctors don't always know what's best— and no one is cutting up my child, even if Medi-Cal is paying every cent.

Most importantly, I learned that in spite of my fears and my loyalty to my dysfunctional husband, I was slowly, bravely, inadvertently, inch by inch, beginning to have the look of a single mother.

Dear White Raven,
It has been so long since I sat here at the beginning of this holy saga of my life. I have come back to drink a coffee, to celebrate, to bid you adieu. This book is coming to a close.

I came here with a headache— the beginning of a long slow labor. And now the only thing that matters is getting it out of me and into the world. And you, White Raven, have allowed the present to embrace the past and make it richer than it was when it was simply being lived.

I wonder how I would have been able to talk of my life, or what it might have had to teach me, without having been written. It was a nebulous swirl of images, some fading and ephemeral, some weighty and sharp as yesterday—my mother at the clothesline, my father in his easy chair with his pipe. Counterculture friends and lovers and ocean voyages; Jerusalem and Paris and the Midwest and the mountains of California. Pain and ecstasy, phantoms and dead people, and childbirth, and love in the wilderness. Now that it is written, it is something to leave behind when I myself become a vaporous memory like the ones I have gathered and kept and that have churned themselves into this story that I wrote and wrote and could not stop writing.

The Wandering Muse—she never deserted me through all those years in the trailer and the half-built house. The beautiful Muse, with sparkling silver hair, has taken a bow and is about to go on leave of absence.

But She will come again when called, as She has always come.

CHAPTER 4

The Song of the House on the Hill

I WAS NOT A CHANTING Buddhist, but if Buddhism is acceptance through the path of struggle—then I was becoming a Buddhist on that hill. The flies that were my nemesis, cause of screaming insanity, were now just flies.

The house did not change. I was what changed. But it was more than change. It was metamorphosis. My childhood in the house on Drummond Road was pre-life, embryonic—a sanctified cocoon. When I fled, raw and unprepared, I began a long pilgrimage, an initiation into struggle and pain. My only regret, alas, is that I pulled my children along on my quest.

Now I accepted everything, and a great sense of peace was taking hold. I owned it all: the beautiful and the ugly, the house that would not change, that was all it would ever be for us—a half-built house. And I began to detach from my husband who was losing his ties not only to the house, but to everything substantial. He had been living inside an inflated dream, and the air was slowly seeping out of it.

It was only when I was in the force field of Tom's madness that I felt unstable and uncertain. It was hard to escape that, and the children too were vulnerable and scared.

I had taken on a motherly attitude toward my husband and toward the house itself, crying with it as it spilled long drips of tears into cans and buckets. But, in nature, sometimes a mother has to leave behind a dying child. A mother elephant with a herd of young, leaves her sick calf in the savanna, and moves on.

I woke up terrified. . . in and out of a dream.
you were trapping me,
chaining me to the bed
someplace far away. . .medieval
and suddenly I knew
there was a dungeon once
and I was captive there
and we were doing it again
all these years
under a spell
and I was your victim
doing it again
and you, my lord
building this castle

doing it again

In all things there is a spirit that can live and change and thrive and decay. When you walk into a house, a church, a school, a museum, you feel the spirit of that place, the melding of its history and all the people dead and living who entered into it. In all places there is a spirit that defines the place. In the mountains, in the prairies, in the forest, the rivers and the tundra. There is a spirit in all living things and in all things made of once living things. In stone and trees and soil. In the sunrise and the mineral mines and the moon-swept land. The Indians have the knowing and give names to the spirits.

And so it was that the hill that was once just a green meadow barren of trees, where children searched for Easter eggs in the tall wheatgrasses. . so it was, that the spirit of the hill and of the house on the hill became a dying spirit, ghostly and lost.

The house on the hill was stuck in the middle of its own birthing. The father of the house sat in his brown down jacket before the redwood-topped table in the room with rug walls, and rocked to and fro wandering the black, silent spaces among the planets, lost in lives lived long ago when he was someone else. The woman walked solid on the earth, feeling all the woman pain of a birth that is not progressing, feeling the sadness of the rain-warped floor boards, the dank hand-made pillows once made in the house where there was love, the sagging curtains that covered the shelves of old spice jars, littered with the droppings of mice.

And so the sickness of the man and the pain of the woman and the need of the children who were growing into their own ways, could not blend to make the house a thing of substance. And the house became a blemish on the land and the rains came each year, and the thistles grew tall, as tall as a grown man, and they covered the driveway, and the rains washed away the gravel, and the great crevasses that ran along the edges of the drive, carved out by the rivers of rain, became deeper, and the road became uneven and spongy and soft as a pathway through the woods. Nature reclaimed the hill, and the house and all the piles of unused timbers, the bricks, the slate, the wire, the refuse and the rubble: all these were an eyesore, and an abomination.

Amen

CHAPTER 5

Big Puffy Letters In The Sky

"If I am not for myself, then who will be for me? And if I am only for myself, then what am I? And if not now, when?"

-Hillel, The Elder

I had never been much good at decisions, the way an ER doctor makes them when the patient is wheeled in, the way the CEO makes them at a board meeting, or my father, reeling out perfect directives into a dictating machine. I had just drifted, believing in the timing of things, and indecision became a kind of decision, and the crisis resulting from the indecision became the turning. I was swept along, a leaf in the river—a drifter in time. A drifter, and one who patiently waits.

Maybe I had learned patience during the years that I had migraines. I would sit in a chair nearly unconscious, knowing it would be over, waiting for that moment when the pain lifted off and left me light-headed and euphoric.

I waited, knowing that I would leave, just not how or when. I stood at the point where the past, that long winding trail, joins the future, indistinct but charged already with certainty. I would be right there to hear the clink of the joining when my future settled into its course, gathering momentum—a witness to what I already knew would happen.

I had a husband once, and apparently he went crazy. I told him I was afraid for him. He told me that people don't understand the transcendental state. He gave me books to read. He said I would not be to blame if he went too far away and did not come back. He absolved me of responsibility.

He said he needed to be alone, and that if I did not leave with the children, he would have to leave. He told me I should go out into the world and be beautiful again.

Tom told the men at Recycled Construction that he was going to levitate the timbers of our house into place. He told this to strangers. I know. I was there. He told his children that he could make things move by willing them to move, that he was learning to fly. That he might one day become invisible—disappear.

My old high school friend, Sandra, came from Marin with her daughter, now six. It was thirteen years since she took me to the party in Berkeley where I met Tom Corn in his purple paisley sweater. After her husband Bob returned from Viet Nam his practice in psychiatry flourished, and they now lived a picture-perfect life in Mill Valley. Walking up the hill in the 80-degree heat she took it all in: the rubbish pile, the tattered mattress on the garage floor, the old bags of dried cement.

We walked up the steps. The rug walls. The Wedgewood stove hooked to a five-gallon propane tank. The food shelves covered by cheap Woolworth fabric. The torn mylar windows. She kept her daughter close to her, as if afraid that she would be electrocuted by a loose wire or fall off the edge of the living room without walls.

Then, she saw him sitting in his place on the floor in his brown down jacket patched with duct tape, rocking, rocking. He began to rattle on, and he didn't stop until it was time for her to go.

Down below, clutching her daughter in one hand and grabbing my hand with the other, she said, "Laurie, I've known you a long time, since we were kids. We've gone our separate ways, but I know this isn't you. You are living like a martyr. Why?"

I answered, facetiously, "No, I am not a martyr anymore. I am well into my sainthood now."

"And how long has Tom been like this? He's flippy. He needs help. If you love him, get him to a hospital. Come and talk to Bob. He's a psychiatrist. He can help you."

"I know it's serious, but I'm not sure that's the right thing to do. Sometimes he's okay, milking the goats, walking to town. Other times he's way out there, telling people he's learning to levitate things. I'm not sure yet what to do, but the men in white coats? I don't think so. I'm afraid for him, but shock therapy? It isn't right for him. He would never forgive me."

"Then ask other people. Get advice. Call me."

I asked the Buddhists and they said he was safe in a community where he was cared for. They offered to hold a healing *pujah* at Vajrapani.

I asked Charles who said: "He's no more crazy than the rest of us. He's just seeing more. He's finding his way out of where he was and he'll never be the same. He needs to be alone for a while. You are a precious flower. Take care of yourself."

I asked his mother, and she said: "Isn't there a therapist he can see?"

And then I asked a stranger on an airplane, because once in a while in an airplane when you have a real thing on your mind, you get beyond the airplane talk—"Are you from Chicago or just visiting there?"—and you spill everything on your mind, and you get a blessing from a nameless traveler 30,000 feet up in the sky.

The stranger sitting next to me, a nice businessman in a suit, listened to my story and said, "You seem like a compassionate and intelligent woman. Trust yourself. You'll do the right thing at the right time." I looked out the window, half expecting to see them: big puffy letters in the sky spelling THE END.

CHAPTER 6

The Spell

I HAD BEEN TRAPPED IN the alchemy of a strange and powerful soul connection. Milton the psychic said he did not see a strong future picture of me and Tom. My genie, David, had once reminded me that my children came first. But my husband was my child too, and as fragile as a newborn. He underwent a transfiguration; he no longer lived in his body, and it was in the physical that we knew one another. The physical, for us, had been the gateway to the soul. I looked at him now, and saw a stranger—a strange, strange man.

Charles had once told me that Tom and I were good if we weren't talking, that if we never said another word to one another we would be fine. Maybe that was meant to be tongue-in-cheek, but I think there is a terrible truth in what he said; I think it is pathetically true. Now the spell was broken, and I had fresh gumption, was no longer the loyal, helpless helpmeet of the man on the hill. I was already a single mother of two.

We women—especially intuitive introverts who happen to be writers, are receivers, receptacles, literally. For us, there may not be a visible light at the end of a tunnel that turns this way and that, sometimes muddy, sometimes clear. We observe, absorb. We find our way through the tunnel without even knowing it, in the end making sense out of what looks like chaos. Maybe we writers simply stay in the story because we need to see what happens—see how the story ends. . .

CHAPTER 7

Came The Flood

AND THIS IS HOW IT ends: It was 1982, the year of the great flood that buried roads and washed away schools. People were crushed to death as their houses lost their footings and slid with the mud, and crumbled into creeks. Houses and parts of houses rushed down the San Lorenzo River as if they had someplace to go.

I missed Trina. She no longer lived in the log cabin behind us, so I drove to Capitola by the Sea to the coffee shop where she worked. Mr. Toots was a popular espresso place for artists and writers. It was on the second floor above Margaritaville on the Esplanade. All the way there, for some inexplicable reason, I kept envisioning Milton, the past-life psychic—wishing for him, but he lived in Los Gatos twenty miles away. I walked up the steps to Mr. Toots. Trina who was behind the coffee bar came over to me and sat down.

"I need to do something. Tom is flipped out and I'm trying hard not to get drawn in. One night he made me think I was Van Gogh in a past life and I started to believe it. And now he's telling the kids that he's learning the secret of becoming invisible."

Before she could say a word, Milton was sitting across from me. He had just walked up the stairs with a young woman and when he spotted me he drifted over to our table and dropped into a chair. I was dizzy, breathless, seeing him at my table, gripped by the surreal sense that I was no longer adrift, waiting for things to happen. The air was charged; the rapid pounding of my heart was the sound of destiny galloping toward me like a winged horse. All I had to do was stay out of its way.

Milton reached across the table, put his hand over mine and said, "My dear, you are in crisis. Do whatever you can to get out of the house, now. Tom is better off alone. It's what he wants. If you have to go on welfare, do it. If you have friends or family to go to, go to them. You are a strong woman, but his energetic field is dangerous. Protect yourself and your kids; stay out of his way."

The skies poured for days. Our house was the deck of the Titanic and the sea was swallowing it as rain followed torrential rain. Our house was the abandoned hulk of a great ship, and the captain was going down with the ship.

In the Flood of 1982, Fall Creek which ran through the famous dining hall of the Brookdale Lodge, had run amuck and washed away the hall. Federal funding was on the way, but the Lodge needed cash and they were renting out rooms to displaced people.

One day Sami Bird whispered to me, "Daddy said he's learning to fly."

"Okay Sami Bird, but we are flying too. We are flying away for awhile." And so we flew, just the three of us: Sami, Ben, and I—to the Brookdale Lodge because we were displaced. Tom wanted to be alone, so we left him on the hill with nothing to eat but apples from a nearby orchard and his precious goat's milk to drink.

There, in a room of the Brookdale Lodge, began our new life. I had no plan, no idea of what we would do next. We'd make it up as we went along. I felt the kind of elation you feel after surviving a disaster. We were safe. My kids still had all their toes and fingers, and there was a big future out there latching onto all three of us like a thick rescue rope, beginning its pull.

We made the room our own, pushing the two beds together so the children would not fight over who would sleep with me. I put my typewriter on the table in the corner. We took the clown pictures off the wall, put up one of my drawings. I bought a red cooler and a hot plate for coffee and oatmeal.

One day Tom came to visit us at the Lodge. I was sitting on the outside balcony of our upstairs room and saw his tall lean form loping through the parking lot in that stony, weightless walk of his. He came into the room, his face flushed and excited. He had worked out a way of winning at the horse races, he said. He figured it out mathematically, based on astral conjunctions. He said he would be taking care of us when the million dollars came through. And then he turned and bounded away.

At the Brookdale Lodge

On the dial of the thermostat are the tiny words
'comfort zone'
There is a bar downstairs, but
I am keeping to myself
The San Francisco of our Love
The Zone Called Paradise
is one thousand light years away

We three have settled like refugees
into the Comfort Zone

To Tom I type:
It is better to be here, longing
to be with you
than to be there, longing
to be away from you
with no place to go

I had a husband once.
I am a single mother now

The End

(big puffy letters in the sky)

EPILOGUE

The Housewarming On China Grade Road

Boulder Creek, California
1992

My father, eighty-one, trudged heroically by my side, past the parked cars at the bottom, around the switchback, and up the steepest part of the graveled drive to the house at the top. The driveway, after all these years, was still not paved and continued to go back to nature in the winter rains.

In 1984 Tom and I agreed to sell our land, and a woman named Beverly bought the half-built house and all the salvaged materials. She was the only one brave enough to take it on. She loved the land, and had horses stabled down below and pedigreed Saluki dogs up above sharing her home.

I was invited to Beverly's housewarming and asked my father to come. He had moved west after the death of my mother. I hadn't been up on that hill since fleeing with the children in 1982, the year of the flood. In the past ten years the horses had grazed the land, eating up the tall blond wheat grasses that once covered the hill. Native bushes took over, tough as wire, spreading across the rising meadow like dark, alien blemishes.

Beverly met us at the door. In the foyer lay some of the large slabs of slate flooring bequeathed to her as part of the sale—once pried loose by Tom and me from a bath house in up-scale Atherton for the hearth of our future living room. We were ushered inside to the main room, much smaller than the spacious living room of our plans. The over-sized windows so carefully designed by Tom to capture the full scope of the mountain vista were smaller, cropping the tops of the farthest ridges.

This was a cozy home, not crazy with size, not a monument boasting masculine grandeur, but a modest house, enough for a single woman—a living room with an adequate view, a small bedroom, a sewing room, and a functional kitchen. It was a conventional house that could have been placed anywhere—on a suburban street, on a country road, nothing that would turn your head. Not a fortress towering above the simple country homes down below.

We sat in the living room among Beverly's friends who had helped her complete the house, through work parties, in eight years. She had kept the rounded shape of Tom's master plan more or less, as the concrete foundation was already in place, but the two rounded sections facing the mountains (our living room and kitchen with a view) were truncated and reduced in breadth.

Do you smell a bit of arrogance, sense the taste of sour grapes? It is not so. I knew full well that Tom's dream house was the vision of a dreamer. Yet, the impossible dream still clung, a bittersweet image in my mind. It was, after all, Beverly who finished the house. It may have been half-there by lofty mountain standards, but it was not half-done. It was finished—colorful curtains and all.

And what became of Tom Corn when the land was sold? He had sat up there on the hill for two years, a hermit asking little of the world and getting what he needed: space and solitude. He had survived on goat's milk, peanut butter, and apples from a nearby orchard.

I had finally come to understand how all those women did it. They walked away, putting one foot in front of the other. Because my husband had become a stranger to me I was able to be one of those women; the spell was broken. Yet when I looked at old pictures of him and me, I felt the familiar pull, the longing, and sometimes I would trek up our hill to sit and talk, to see if he was all right.

It's probably good that Tom never saw this house in its Devolved version. When he abandoned the hill, he never returned. His vision of the majestic mountain home would live there in his somewhat paralyzed psyche forever. The sale of the land afforded us enough to pay my father what he had lent us over the years, left me enough to pay for a rented house north of Boulder Creek, and gave Tom enough cash to buy himself a Datsun 510 station wagon that he lived in for two years. He parked it in various spots in town, at times near Boulder Creek Elementary where Sami sometimes passed it on her way to school.

Tom, at least outwardly, had drifted back to earth, got a job as tour guide at the Mystery Spot in Santa Cruz where the trees twisted like corkscrews and birds did not settle; where light beams did tricky things—where if a tall man and a short woman traded places on a level concrete slab, the woman would mysteriously appear taller than the man.

He worked there by day, eventually managed the gift shop, and lived in a shed on the property where he cooked his meals in an electric wok. He continued pumping up revelations at the apex of the crooked Mystery Spot house where the force was the strongest. Tom was successful at his work, yet he persisted in the belief that he was immortal, that he was exempt from dying. Over time he lowered that expectation; he would live until the age of two hundred. His mind was always busy with past life connections. When Lenore had a baby he was excited to announce that the baby was his grandfather, a violinist, reincarnated. Strangely, when she grew up, this child became singer-songwriter.

There was a softness and a sadness about Tom. His solitude was due more to circumstance than choice. He had lost his family. I found out, years after we left him alone on the hill, that he had not meant for our separation to be forever; he had expected that we'd get back together as a family. It saddened me to know this, but I was far beyond any thought of reconciliation. The spell was too far broken, and I was far too busy being single.

The four Corns would be together at Christmastime, visiting my in-laws in Rancho Palos Verdes in southern California; there, we were the semblance of a family. Phyllis, Tom's mother, was a paraplegic in her last years. She had been a mild-mannered woman, but now that she had lost control of her ordered life, she was reduced to a world of details. Great energy went into the militant placement of things on the table next to her bed. Everything, to the millimeter, in its exact place.

She was a woman in denial, pretending we were a couple, believing that if her son would just go back to Lockheed, get a real job, things would be as they were before. As if I were his wife, she'd say to me on the side: "Can't you get Tommy to cut his hair?"

Sami became one of the thousands of young women bereft of a healthy father-daughter relationship. In her community college days she stayed with Tom for a time in his shack at the Mystery Spot, riding her bike there after classes. She wanted to have a father. Benjamin too wanted that; he called his dad often to discuss science questions.

Today Ben takes care of the elderly, the disabled, and people with dementia. Sami is a massage practitioner and is studying to become a counselor. My children have become healers.

After the Brookdale Lodge where this story ended, my kids and I moved around the small towns of the San Lorenzo Valley: at first in a home we shared with a crazy lady who slept with the propane man when her tank needed a refill; once in a leaky trailer; and for a while up the mountain at Omland with Tamar and Charles.

Remember when Tom Corn told me to go back into the world to be beautiful again? I needed no coaxing. I fell into men—good men, some Buddhist, some not so Buddhist. But that is another story. . .

When the merry-go-round of men wound down to a stop, I became a recluse. I needed to live ten years alone to get reacquainted with My Laurie Me, that small girl in the closet at Breldway who had found her core strength at age four. I was steadily, inadvertently becoming a woman who would never let submissiveness or love addiction define me again. And so, once upon a time. . .

In 2009, I met Dick Harrah, a widower of ten years, who was himself born and raised in Toledo! (Was Toledo the nexus of the world?) He had followed his hero Jack Kerouac's example and hitched across the country more than once, finally settling in California. He was a brilliant Yale graduate who was a beloved teacher of high school students for forty years.

We fell into goony love in our seventies. He was a slim elfin man, stunning white hair falling sideways across his forehead—like Andy Warhol. Dick Harrah, a pagan at heart, was at home with the many Greek gods and goddesses of mythology. He said that we humans have it better than the gods. They could not experience perfervid passion, the miracle of finding a soul mate, the finality and inevitability of their demise because they were, *helas*, immortal. Humans get to have it all: birth, passion, pain, death, AND transcendental moments of immortality. He would say—in moments of heightened pleasure or when we were sitting four feet from one another and feeling the palpable force between us, "You know that we are touching the eternal." We humans, unlike the gods, get to be mortal *and* immortal.

He invited me to come live with him in his "mysteriously remote romantic mountain hide-away." There were gardens, a bistro table in the back where we would drink a glass of wine in the dusk of day, looking out on the Santa Cruz Mountains. Our home was dedicated to love. It was a gift to live like that. I experienced what I had always believed—that relationship can be easy. I learned what a couple can be when there is mutual respect, appreciation, admiration, and burning love. He was a mystic, a mythologist, a gifted bard writing his own epic poems—and in the end, a fatalist. We had six scintillating, love-drenched years before he succumbed to cancer and moved on to, what he called, "the next great adventure."

At the memorial one of his young students called me a widow and I recoiled. Wasn't a widow an old Greek woman shrouded in black with a veil over her cracked face?

In the 80s, at a meeting of the Center for World Networking, a spiritual community in Santa Cruz, Tom met a woman named Maria who became his partner for the next twenty years. They moved to Asheville, North Carolina, where Tom worked for the school district, attending to special needs children on the school buses. The giant Bozak speakers lived in their home where he sat cross-legged, absorbed in his music.

Eventually, Tom went into mental decline and when Maria could no longer care for him, Ben moved his dad to Bellingham where he lives with his wife, Roxanne. At the time of this writing, Tom Corn, at seventy-five, resides in a memory care facility in the last stages of dementia. I wonder where that brilliant mind has taken him. Is he out there beyond the earthly plane in some sphere familiar only to himself, or is he lost—his brain an impossible tangle? Strange to think that he who sat in a trance listening to Schoenberg's "Transfigured Night" is, himself, at the threshold of the ultimate transfiguration.

As the housewarming on China Grade continued, Beverly's friends sat around eating refreshments, trading stories, and applauding their accomplishments. I had this glorified fantasy that I had been invited because I was, after all, the legendary first lady of the hill. They would sit at my feet and I would read from my poetry that authenticated the rich hippie history attached to every piece of slate, every large beam, every slab of redwood. I would read to them, and my dad would be proud.

But I was mistaken. For her friends, the history of the house began when she bought it from some people (us), and they were gathered now to celebrate Beverly's new home and their part in it. I was truly a ghost.

You will remember the famous timber salvaged from the Downieville mill, that twenty-two-foot-long twelve-by-twelve post that was to be the center of the spoke wheel of beams in the living room. That huge timber never stayed in Beverly's house. It was removed and deposited in the grasses like an abandoned afterthought. One young man looked out the window down the hill, spotted the timber, and said to Beverly, "That big piece of wood down there, I could get you a good price for it if you wanted." A piece of wood detached forever from its primary purpose. Its destiny, instead, would be to live in a book.

About the spoke wheel of beams that was supposed to radiate out from the center post, Tom had confessed years later that he was afraid of the welding, that he feared electricity, and that's what had held him up. So why didn't he just hire someone, you might ask. Well, in all fairness, why did I not just hire someone to hook up the hot water heater? I was just as hung up, thinking that I was helpless to make things happen. So much hot water under the bridge.

Mrs. Howard, the daughter of old Mrs. Crawford who had sold us the land in 1972, approached me. She was seemingly our nemesis all those years. She and her husband were the ones filing complaints. We had never actually talked to one another; to me, she was the mean tattletale across the street. She smiled and said that she was so happy I was in better circumstances. She seemed a kind woman, genteel and gracious. She assured me that she never meant to harm us, but was trying to help the children and me by bringing our difficult situation to the attention of the county. Ah, so! We exchanged pleasantries and wished each other well.

I thanked Beverly, stepped out the door, stood a moment gazing at the redwood mountains, turned my back on the house, walked slowly down the hill with my eighty-one-year-old father, got into my car, and drove away.

AFTERWORD

MILTON, THE PAST-LIFE PSYCHIC, TOLD me that my work in this life was to learn to be with a man without being dependent on him and without his being dependent on me. My life work? Back then I thought that was ludicrous. I wanted my money back.

I had misunderstood. He did not say it was my life *purpose*; it was my *work*. And now I know that he was right. As for Tom Corn and me—ours was an epic love, fraught with passion, adventure, dreams, madness, ruin, and, for me, redemption. It was "my work in this life." Dick Harrah and I were a mature and worldly pair when we fell into goony love. We brought our best selves to the table, and we feasted. We touched the eternal. That white-haired elfin man has completed my life—so far.

Made in the USA
San Bernardino, CA
16 January 2020

62863393R00190